LOVINA EICHER'S AMI.

# AMISH
## FAMILY RECIPES

"Oh, do I ever love cookbooks, especially those with time-honored Amish recipes! *Amish Family Recipes* is one you will cherish for years to come and will pass down to the next generation of cooks in your own family."
—**Beverly Lewis**, *New York Times* bestselling author of Amish fiction

"Open this book and time slows down. Lovina will take you on a food journey you don't want to miss out on. You'll find delicious recipes and short stories to remind you of what really matters in life—relationships and sharing nourishing food with those you love."
—**Hope Helmuth**, author of *Hope's Table: Everyday Recipes from a Mennonite Kitchen*

"This cookbook is amazing, with beautiful photography, recipes that are simple to follow, unique foods that don't include unusual ingredients. Real Amish cooking at its best!"
—**Linda Byler**, bestselling author of *Sadie's Montana* Amish fiction trilogy

"Open Lovina Eicher's newest cookbook, *Amish Family Recipes*, and you'll find yourself transfixed by the welcome it extends to her farm, her life, and to her kitchen. Stunning photography accompanies mouthwatering recipes, but a favorite feature will be the "tidbit" sidebars of Lovina's family life. This will be a keeper."
—**Suzanne Woods Fischer**, award-winning author of Amish fiction and non-fiction

LOVINA EICHER'S AMISH KITCHEN

# AMISH
# FAMILY RECIPES

**A COOKBOOK ACROSS *the* GENERATIONS**

## Lovina Eicher

**HERALD**
PRESS

Harrisonburg, Virginia

Herald Press
PO Box 866, Harrisonburg, VA 22803
www.HeraldPress.com

**Library of Congress Cataloging-in-Publication Data**
Names: Eicher, Lovina, author.
Title: Amish family recipes : a cookbook across the generations / Lovina Eicher.
Description: Harrisonburg, Virginia : Herald Press, 2020. | Includes index.
Identifiers: LCCN 2019045833 (print) | LCCN 2019045834 (ebook) |
    ISBN 9781513805771 (paperback) | ISBN 9781513805788 (ebook)
Subjects: LCSH: Amish cooking. | Cooking, American. | LCGFT: Cookbooks.
Classification: LCC TX721 .E352 2020  (print) | LCC TX721  (ebook) |
    DDC 641.5/66—dc23
LC record available at https://lccn.loc.gov/2019045833
LC ebook record available at https://lccn.loc.gov/2019045834


AMISH FAMILY RECIPES
© 2020 by Herald Press, Harrisonburg, Virginia 22803. All rights reserved.
Library of Congress Control Number: 2019045833
International Standard Book Number: 978-1-5138-0577-1 (paperback);
    978-1-5138-0578-8 (ebook)
Printed in United States of America
Cover and interior design by Merrill Miller
Cover photos by Grant Beachy
Interior photos by Grant Beachy
Additional photos by Merrill Miller and Getty Images
Food arranging by Jennifer Beachy

Writings from Elizabeth Coblentz appeared in her syndicated newspaper column
and in Elizabeth Coblentz, *The Best of the Amish Cook*, vols. 1–2, ed. Kevin
Williams. Selected writings from Lovina Eicher appeared in her syndicated
newspaper column and in Lovina Eicher, *The Best of the Amish Cook*, vols. 3–4,
ed. Kevin Williams.

24 23 22 21 20      10 9 8 7 6 5 4 3 2 1

*To the many generations of cooks in my family—grandmothers, aunts, Mother, sisters, daughters, and granddaughters—and to all the men in the family who enjoy helping with the cooking and enjoy eating the food we make.*

# CONTENTS

*Acknowledgments* • 13

*Introduction* • 15

1. Breakfast and Brunch • 22

2. Breads and Rolls • 42

3. Soups and Sandwiches • 62

4. Meats and Main Dishes • 80

5. Vegetables, Sides, and Salads • 104

6. Cakes and Pies • 126

7. Cookies • 146

8. Desserts • 166

9. Miscellaneous • 184

10. Family Picnics • 198

11. Family Reunion Meals • 210

12. Cooking with Children • 222

*Index* • 233

*The Author* • 255

# ACKNOWLEDGMENTS

*S*pecial thanks to my family for always helping and encouraging me to keep writing my columns, and for writing the column in my place some weeks. I appreciate my family helping to prepare and test recipes and all that goes with making this cookbook possible.

Thank you to my husband, Joe, of twenty-six years, my daughter Elizabeth (age 25), and her husband, Tim, and their children, Abigail Elizabeth (age 3), Timothy Josiah (T. J.; age 1), and newborn Allison Lovina. My daughter Susan (age 24) and her husband, Mose, and their children, Jennifer Susan (2), and Ryan Isaiah (8 months). Also thank you to my daughters Verena (age 22), Loretta (19), and Lovina (15), and my sons Benjamin (20), Joseph (17), and Kevin (14). Thank you to Loretta's special friend of three years, Dustin. I love each of them so much and love cooking for all of them when they are all here. I feel truly blessed to call them my family.

I also want to express sincere thanks to a very special friend of mine, Ruth Boss. Without her help this book would still not be finished. She has done so much for me and my family since we met her years ago. Thank you to those who tested the recipes and helped Ruth, namely Judy Alderden, Dawn Borgman, Tricia Boss, Jana Brandenburger, Laura De Young, and Jori Pittman.

—*Lovina Eicher*

# LOVINA AND JOE EICHER FAMILY

# INTRODUCTION

*M*y dear mother died suddenly seventeen years ago. She is still greatly missed but left us a great legacy of memories and all her recipes. For over ten years she had penned a cooking column for newspapers across the country, and after her death I began writing in her place. For a dozen years my column was called The Amish Cook. During that time, I coauthored cookbooks under that name, including *The Amish Cook at Home*, *The Amish Cook's Baking Book*, *The Amish Cook's Anniversary Book*, and *Amish Cooks across America*. After publishing these books, I joined the team at Herald Press, which syndicates my weekly column under its new name, Lovina's Amish Kitchen, and I still write for them. I am blessed to have such great Christian editors to help keep me writing and publishing my cookbooks. In 2017 my first cookbook without a coauthor was published, *The Essential Amish Cookbook*, and many copies have been sold. It is available from Herald Press, Amazon, or your local bookstore.

I was born May 22, 1971, to my wonderful parents, Ben and Elizabeth Coblentz, and I am now forty-eight years old. My husband, Joe (age 51), and I have been married twenty-six years. In 2004 we moved, along with six children, from Indiana to our home in southwest Michigan. We are now blessed with eight children—five girls and three boys. Two of our daughters are married, and we have five grandchildren. Our life does not have a dull moment, and it seems to get busier all the time!

My family has many recipes that have been handed down from generation to generation. I make the same bread recipe my grandmother and mother used to make, for example. Now my daughters follow in our footsteps and use the same recipe when they bake bread. When I first read the recipe, it read like this:

*1 pack yeast*

*Warm water*

*Salt*

*Sugar*

*Lard the size of an egg*

*Bread flour*

*Mix until an elastic dough and bake until golden.*

This can be very confusing for a beginner cook. Gradually, through the generations, exact written measurements and baking instructions were added to the recipe. This makes it much easier for new cooks to also enjoy it! It is included in my last book, *The Essential Amish Cookbook.*

As a young girl I went over to Grandma and Grandpa's house to help them with whatever needed to be done. I often helped my grandmother prepare a meal. She had no refrigeration other than her cool cellar, so she had milk brought in every day from the cows my uncle and aunt milked. Grandma kept the milk cold by setting it in cold water, which was changed often. All her food, such as meats and vegetables, was canned in jars and stored in the cellar. Meat that wasn't canned was sugar cured and had to be used up before the warm days came. Summer sausage was smoked to keep it longer. My parents also used sugar to cure their hams and bacon. Dad would smoke our summer sausage in the smokehouse he built.

Grandma would never have cooked recipes like pizza, taco salad, burritos, and so on. One time when she was at our house we made pizza for supper. Back then our pizza was made by using bread slices for the crust, ketchup for the sauce, and ground beef for the meat. Grandma said pizza was not food to her and so she wouldn't eat it, and frowned upon us eating it.

For the first few years of their marriage, Mother kept the food cold during the summer months by setting it in a barrel that Dad had buried in the ground. A few years later, Mother had a cooler in the basement in which she kept a fifty-pound block of ice, along with the food that was to stay cold. We had to buy the ice at the icehouse. There were big ice tongs hanging inside to lift the ice block and put it in our cooler. Then we wrapped the cooler in blankets to shade it from the sun as we drove the eight miles home in an open buggy. Eventually, it became easier to get ice after there was an ice and phone shed close to our house, and we could buy ice from the freezers there. The calls we made on the phone had to be written down and cost twenty-five cents for each call, plus the long-distance charge that was billed to us each month. Finally, the iceman had the Amish put our coolers by the road with the money inside for however many blocks of ice we needed for the week. He would deliver the ice to everyone.

Fast-forward to how we live since our move to Michigan. We have a propane refrigerator. My children and grandchildren will never know how hard it was to keep our food cold years ago, although a lot of Amish settlements still use blocks of ice to keep food cold. I was really excited when I had my first refrigerator and hot and cold running water! Life was so much easier raising a family this way. Thank you, however, to my ancestors for teaching me how hard life can be, and how we can do without things if we have to!

Many recipes in this book have been made over and over throughout the years, and we also enjoy trying out new ones. We bring this new book to all of you who enjoy working in the kitchen. We have included some outdoor recipes for when it's too nice to cook inside the house. Joe and several of our children, our sons-in-law, and Loretta's special friend all enjoy cooking on the grill. I never complain when they give me a break from cooking! It's nice sometimes to sit back and relax and eat the food right as it comes off the grill.

*Amish Family Recipes: A Cookbook across the Generations* was made to honor all the cooks before and after me in my precious family. May God bless each of you as you enjoy foods from generations ago, and also new foods from the present. Happy cooking, my friends!

# Breakfast & Brunch

*We like trying different ways to make breakfast. If I have leftover hard-cooked eggs from a previous meal, this is a great way to use them.*

## BACON AND EGG BAKE

**6–8 bacon slices**
**1 medium onion, sliced**
**1 (10½-ounce) can cream of mushroom soup**
**¼ cup milk**
**5 hard-cooked eggs, grated**
**2 cups shredded cheese**
**Pepper**

Fry bacon until crisp; remove from pan, drain, and crumble. Sauté onion in bacon drippings, then mix all ingredients together, seasoning with pepper as desired. Pour into a greased baking dish and bake at 350°F for 25–30 minutes. Serve over toasted bread or toasted English muffins.

*This is a great recipe for those who like their eggs hard-cooked instead of made another way.*

## GOLDENROD EGGS

**3 tablespoons butter**

**⅓ cup all-purpose flour**

**2 cups milk**

**½ teaspoon salt**

**4 slices toast**

**8 hard-cooked eggs, sliced**

Make a white sauce by combining butter, flour, milk, and salt in a skillet. Boil just until thickened. Arrange toast on plate, then pour white sauce over toast and top with sliced eggs.

Makes 2–4 servings.

**My mom** used to poach eggs for me after I had a baby, because she said fried food wasn't good for nursing mothers. My daughter Susan remembers them looking so good that she wanted to take them away from me. I made poached eggs when Susan had her second baby.

*This is a great way to make a quick and hearty breakfast. Since we have our own chickens and raise our own pigs, we often enjoy eggs, bacon, and sausage for breakfast.*

## EGG OMELET

**8 eggs**
**½ cup milk or water**
**1 teaspoon salt**
**⅛ teaspoon black pepper**
**1 cup fried and chopped sausage or bacon**
**⅓ cup chopped green bell pepper**
**2 tablespoons butter**
**⅓ cup shredded cheese**

Beat eggs slightly with milk or water, then add salt and pepper. Add meat and bell pepper. Melt butter in a skillet; pour egg mixture in pan and cook over low heat. As omelet cooks, lift edges with spatula and tilt pan to allow uncooked portion to flow underneath. When almost done, sprinkle cheese over top. Continue cooking until omelet is set, then loosen edges with spatula. Crease omelet across center and fold in half. Serve immediately.

Makes 4–6 servings.

**On Christmas** we often have a big brunch, then snack the rest of the day. One of our favorites is "haystack breakfast." We put all the ingredients in bowls, then pass the bowls around the table, with people piling whatever they want on their plates, making a haystack. We have biscuits, scrambled eggs, bacon, ham, onions, green bell peppers, cheese, and gravy.

*This was my cousin's recipe. I like trying new breakfast casseroles and sometimes add ingredients that I think would make it better. I don't make any changes to this recipe—we enjoy it just the way it is.*

## BREAKFAST BRUNCH

**8 eggs**
**1¾ cups milk**
**½ cup flour**
**2 tablespoons dried parsley**
**½ teaspoon dried basil**
**3 cups shredded mozzarella cheese**
**3 cups shredded cheddar cheese**
**2 cups diced ham**
**½ cup chopped green onion**
**½ cup chopped green bell pepper**
**1 (4-ounce) can sliced mushrooms**

In a large bowl, beat together eggs, milk, flour, parsley, and basil. Add cheeses, ham, green onion, bell pepper, and mushrooms, and stir until combined. Place in a well-greased 9 x 13-inch pan. Bake, uncovered, at 350°F for 35–40 minutes.

*This is a family favorite, and of course I double or triple the recipe to make a big roasterful for when the whole family comes for a brunch. It can be made ahead of time so it's ready to put in the oven the next morning.*

## BREAKFAST CASSEROLE WITH WHITE SAUCE

**1 pound meat (ham or sausage works well)**
**1 onion, chopped**
**8 eggs, scrambled and cooked**
**4 large potatoes, shredded**
**1½ pounds cheese, shredded**

**White sauce**
**¼ cup (½ stick) butter**
**¼ cup flour**
**1¾ cups sour cream**
**Salt**

If using cooked ham, cut into cubes. If using sausage, cook in a saucepan with onion and set aside.

To make white sauce, combine all ingredients in a saucepan, seasoning with salt as desired, and heat until thickened.

Layer meat, onion (if not already combined with meat), eggs, potatoes, and cheese in a greased 9 x 13-inch pan, and cover with white sauce. Bake at 400°F for 40 minutes.

### SEPTEMBER 1999, ELIZABETH COBLENZ

I have been washing curtains this week. I am also in the middle of processing grapes, 104 quarts, which will be good to have this winter to drink. Homemade grape juice is always good with breakfast. Grapes are usually ripe in early fall and make excellent juice and jelly.

*We enjoy omelets, and instead of making each one individually we use this recipe to make it easier when we are cooking for the family. By raising our own chickens we always have plenty of eggs, so sometimes we even make this for supper.*

## BREAKFAST OMELET IN A SKILLET

**4 tablespoons butter, divided**
**½ cup diced onion**
**½ cup diced green bell pepper**
**½ cup diced fresh mushrooms**
**2 cups cooked and shredded potatoes**
**1 cup sliced sausage links or ham**
**1 dozen eggs**
**2 teaspoons salt**
**½ cup shredded cheddar cheese**
**Salsa**

In a skillet, melt 2 tablespoons butter. Add onion, bell pepper, and mushrooms, and sauté 5 minutes. Add potatoes and meat. Add the remaining 2 tablespoons butter and allow to melt. In a bowl, beat together eggs and salt, then pour into the skillet. Continue stirring with a spatula over medium heat until almost done (do not completely finish cooking the eggs). Remove from heat and cover skillet; the eggs will continue to cook. Let stand 5 minutes; use spatula to fold the eggs into an omelet shape. Sprinkle cheese on top. Serve with salsa.

*I use muffin liners for this recipe so the muffin pan is easier to wash. If we have overnight guests, this is an easy way to make them a tasty breakfast.*

## CHEESY BAKED EGGS

**½ pound bacon or ham, chopped**
**12 tablespoons milk**
**12 eggs**
**Salt**
**12 tablespoons shredded cheese**

If using bacon, cook bacon in skillet; drain and crumble. Grease muffin pan (or line with muffin liners). Put 1 tablespoon milk, 1 egg, and a pinch salt in each muffin cup. Break up eggs with fork and stir slightly to combine with milk and salt. Top each egg with a little bacon or ham and 1 tablespoon shredded cheese. Bake at 350°F for 15–18 minutes until set.

**One Easter**, Joe took some of the colored eggs we'd made and put them in the chicken coop. Then he sent the boys and their cousin Jacob out to gather the eggs. They came running back hollering, "The chickens laid colored eggs, they know it's Easter too!"

*I like to make this omelet on a weekend morning and serve it with sausage gravy. My husband, Joe, brought this recipe home from work quite a few years ago. A coworker had this in his lunch, and Joe asked for the recipe.*

## BREAKFAST OMELET ROLL

**4 ounces cream cheese, softened**

**¾ cup milk**

**2 tablespoons flour**

**¼ teaspoon salt**

**12 eggs**

**2 tablespoons prepared mustard**

**1½ cups shredded cheese (cheddar or your choice), divided**

**1 pound bacon, fried and chopped**

**1 cup chopped ham**

**¼ cup minced onion**

**¼ cup chopped green bell pepper**

**Additional fillings as desired, such as mushrooms, olives, smoked sausage**

Preheat oven to 375°F. Cut parchment paper to line a 10 x 15-inch jelly-roll pan.

In a large bowl, combine cream cheese and milk. Whisk until smooth. Add flour and salt. In another bowl, whisk eggs, then add to cream cheese mixture. Pour mixture into parchment-lined pan and bake 30–35 minutes, or until puffy and golden.

Remove pan from oven and spread mustard and half the shredded cheese onto the omelet. Add the bacon, ham, onion, bell pepper, any additional fillings as desired, and most of the remaining cheese. Roll up in jelly-roll fashion, removing paper as you roll. Garnish with remaining cheese. Cut into slices to serve.

*These muffins are nice to make when you need to grab a quick breakfast in the morning. We don't always get to sit down together on busy mornings, such as on Sunday mornings when we are getting ready to leave for church, so it's nice to have something easy that will keep warm in the oven for everyone to eat.*

## SCRAMBLED EGG MUFFINS

½ **pound pork sausage**

12 **eggs**

½ **cup chopped onion**

¼ **cup chopped green bell pepper**

½ **teaspoon salt**

¼ **teaspoon black pepper**

¼ **teaspoon garlic powder**

1 **cup shredded cheddar cheese**

Brown the sausage in a skillet; drain. Beat eggs in a bowl. Add onion, bell pepper, salt, pepper, and garlic powder. Stir in sausage and cheese. Grease two muffin pans or line with muffin liners. Spoon ⅓ cup mixture into each muffin cup. Bake at 350°F for 20–25 minutes, or until a knife inserted in the center of a muffin comes out clean.

Makes 2 dozen muffins.

*We use our own cooked maple syrup instead of buying it from the store. My sons-in-law use the sap from their maple trees to make the syrup.*

## CRUNCHY CRUST FRENCH TOAST

**1 egg**
**⅓ cup milk**
**2 teaspoons sugar**
**⅛ teaspoon ground cinnamon**
**1 cup cornflakes, crushed**
**4 slices bread**
**3 tablespoons butter or margarine**

In a medium bowl or pie pan, whisk egg, milk, sugar, and cinnamon. Place cornflakes in another bowl or pan. Dip bread slices in egg mixture, then in crushed cornflakes. Heat butter in skillet and brown bread slices on both sides. Serve hot with pancake syrup.

*We like to serve our homemade maple syrup with these pancakes, along with sausage patties or sausage links. It is a hearty pancake that will fill you up and keep you well fueled as you go about your morning work.*

## BANANA CORNBREAD PANCAKES

**3 bananas**
**⅓ cup granulated sugar**
**1 firmly packed tablespoon brown sugar**
**2 teaspoons vanilla extract**
**1½ cups milk**
**2 cups cornmeal**
**2 teaspoons baking powder**
**2 teaspoons ground cinnamon**
**1 teaspoon salt**
**Butter, for griddling**

In a large bowl, mash the bananas. Add granulated sugar, brown sugar, and vanilla. Whisk until mixed well. Whisk in milk. Sift together cornmeal, baking powder, cinnamon, and salt. Add to banana mixture and whisk until well combined. Melt a small amount of butter in a skillet over medium heat. Pour in ⅓ cup pancake batter. Cook 3–5 minutes, or until lightly golden brown. Flip and cook 2–3 minutes more on other side. Use additional butter as needed to cook remaining pancakes.

Makes 8 pancakes.

**My mother**, Elizabeth, called rolls "sweet rolls," and we call them "cinnamon rolls." I didn't think mine tasted as good as my mother's, and my daughter Elizabeth doesn't think hers taste as good as mine. She said, "Maybe mine taste like Grandma's!"

*This recipe is a great addition to breakfast! The streusel topping makes it very flavorful, and we enjoy eating this with a cup of coffee or a glass of milk. Plan to make this at least eight hours in advance, as the batter must be refrigerated before baking.*

# OVERNIGHT CINNAMON PECAN COFFEE CAKE

**Coffee cake**
¾ cup (1½ sticks) butter, softened
1 cup granulated sugar
2 large eggs
2 cups all-purpose flour
1 teaspoon baking powder
1 teaspoon baking soda
1 teaspoon ground nutmeg
½ teaspoon salt
1 cup sour cream

**Streusel topping**
¾ firmly packed cup brown sugar
½ cup chopped pecans
1 teaspoon ground cinnamon

For coffee cake: Beat butter and sugar until light and fluffy. Add eggs, one at a time, beating after each addition until combined. In a separate bowl, combine flour, baking powder, baking soda, nutmeg, and salt. Add flour mixture to egg mixture, alternating with sour cream. Beat just until blended. Spread batter into a greased 9 x 13-inch pan.

For streusel topping: In a small bowl, combine streusel topping ingredients. Sprinkle topping over batter. Cover pan with plastic wrap and refrigerate 8 to 18 hours.

Preheat oven to 350°F. Bake 35 minutes, or until a toothpick inserted in the center comes out clean. The cake can be served warm or at room temperature.

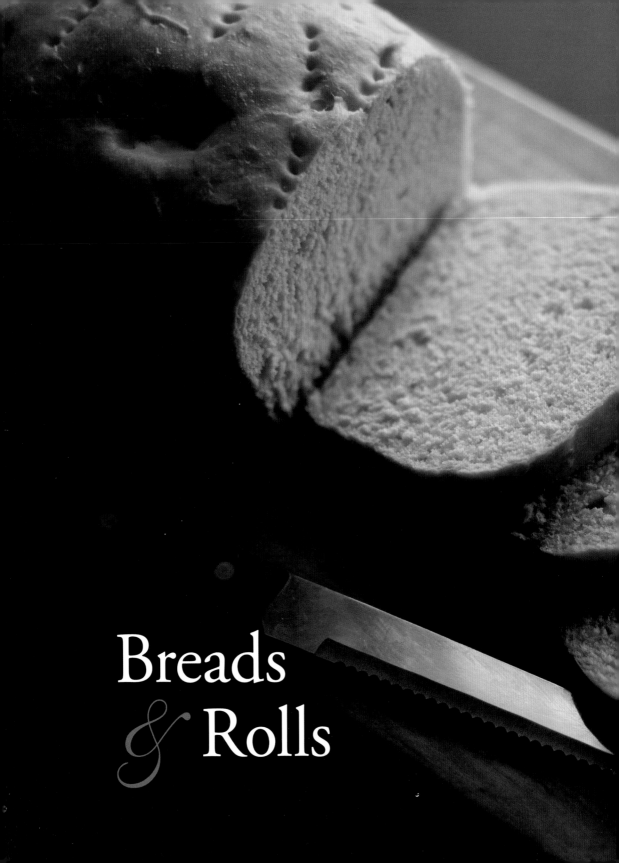

# Breads & Rolls

*We like to eat doughnuts when they are freshly made and still warm. We like to dip them in coffee or a glass of milk.*

## DOUGHNUTS

**2¼ teaspoons (1 package) active dry yeast, or 1 (0.6-ounce) cake compressed yeast**

**¼ cup warm water**

**1 cup scalded milk, cooled**

**2¾ cups unsifted flour, divided**

**1 egg**

**¼ cup shortening**

**⅓ cup granulated sugar**

**1 teaspoon salt**

**1 quart vegetable oil (4 cups)**

**Glaze**

**1 cup confectioners' sugar**

**2 tablespoons milk or water**

Dissolve yeast in water. Add milk and 1 cup flour and mix. Let sponge rise until doubled in size, then add egg, shortening, sugar, and salt. Add remaining 1¾ cups flour and beat using a mixer fitted with a dough hook or by hand using a spoon. Cover and let rise until doubled in size. Turn on floured board and knead lightly. Divide dough in two. Let rest 10 minutes, then press and pat each piece to ½-inch thickness and cut out shapes with doughnut cutter. Let rise again.

In a deep-fryer or large heavy skillet, heat oil to 350°F. Slide doughnuts into the hot oil using a wide spatula. Turn doughnuts over as they rise to the surface. Fry doughnuts on each side until golden brown. Remove from hot oil and drain on a wire rack.

To make glaze, mix confectioners' sugar with milk. Dip warm doughnuts in glaze and set on wire racks to cool. Place baking sheets under the racks for easier cleanup.

*I like this dessert because I usually have everything in the pantry that is needed to make it, and it doesn't take that much time to put together. Our family loves the flavor of caramel, so we really enjoy this dessert.*

## CARAMEL DUMPLINGS

**Sauce**
**1½ cups granulated sugar, divided**
**2 tablespoons butter**
**⅛ teaspoon salt**
**2 cups hot water**

**Dumplings**
**2 tablespoons butter**
**½ cup granulated sugar**
**1 teaspoon vanilla extract**
**1½ cups flour**
**2 teaspoons baking powder**
**½ cup milk**
**Cream or half-and-half, for serving**

To make the sauce, heat ½ cup sugar in a large saucepan until it caramelizes (it will melt and turn brown). Add butter, remaining 1 cup sugar, salt, and water. Cook over medium heat until sugar is dissolved, stirring several times, about 10 minutes.

To make the dumplings, cream together the butter, sugar, and vanilla. Sift together flour and baking powder. Alternate adding milk and flour mixture to the butter mixture, mixing until well combined. Drop batter by spoonful into the saucepan with the sauce. Place over low heat and cook, tightly covered, for about 20 minutes. Serve warm with cream.

*We sprinkle garlic powder on many foods we cook, from meats to vegetables. This bread is good with a meal of spaghetti and meatballs.*

## GARLIC BUBBLE LOAF

¼ cup warm water
2¼ teaspoons (1 package) active dry yeast
2 cups milk
1 tablespoon shortening
2 tablespoons granulated sugar
2 teaspoons salt
5½–6½ cups all-purpose flour

**Garlic butter**
½ cup (1 stick) butter, melted
1 tablespoon dried parsley
2 teaspoons garlic powder

Put warm water in a large mixing bowl. Sprinkle yeast on top and let stand for 5 minutes, or until mixture becomes foamy. Add milk, shortening, sugar, salt, and flour and mix until a sticky dough forms. Turn dough out onto well-floured surface. Knead a few times and put into a large bowl that has been well greased. Turn dough over to coat, then cover bowl lightly with plastic wrap. Let dough rise until doubled, then punch down. Shape dough into little balls.

To make garlic butter, mix together butter, parsley, and garlic powder. Dip balls in garlic butter and place in two greased 9 x 5-inch loaf pans, dividing dough equally between pans. Cover pans and let rise until doubled. Bake at 375°F for 20–30 minutes, or until golden brown.

Makes 2 loaves.

*I started making monkey bread after I had it at one of Joe's uncle and aunt's house for breakfast when we stayed the night with them. It tastes similar to a cinnamon roll but can be sliced or pulled apart to eat.*

## MONKEY BREAD

**1 teaspoon ground cinnamon**

**1¼ cups granulated sugar, divided**

**¾ cup chopped nuts**

**½ cup warm water**

**4½ teaspoons (2 packages) active dry yeast**

**1½ cups lukewarm milk**

**2 eggs**

**½ cup shortening**

**2 teaspoons salt**

**5–7 cups flour**

**¾ cup (1½ sticks) butter, melted**

Mix together cinnamon, ¾ cup sugar, and nuts and set aside.

Measure water and yeast in a large bowl. Stir in remaining ½ cup sugar, milk, eggs, shortening, and salt. Gradually add enough flour until dough is elastic and easy to handle, kneading well. Tear off pieces about the size of a walnut and form into balls. Dip in melted butter, then in cinnamon-sugar mixture. Place in well-greased tube pan and layer until all the dough is used up. Let rise in pan until doubled in size. Pour remaining butter and cinnamon-sugar mixture over dough. Bake at 375°F for 40 minutes. Loosen bread from sides of pan and invert pan onto serving plate.

*After my daughter Elizabeth got married, we were talking about pizza dough recipes. Elizabeth said she really liked her recipe, and I said I really liked mine. When we compared, we discovered we were using the same recipe!*

## MY FAVORITE PIZZA DOUGH

**1 cup warm water**
**1 tablespoon active dry yeast**
**2 tablespoons granulated sugar**
**2 tablespoons vegetable oil**
**1 teaspoon salt**
**2½ cups flour**

In a medium bowl, mix water, yeast, and sugar. Let stand for 10 minutes. Add oil, salt, and flour and mix well. Press dough into a greased 10 x 15-inch jelly-roll pan. Layer on sauce and toppings of your choice and bake at 350°F until crust is golden brown, about 30 minutes.

### SEPTEMBER 1994, ELIZABETH COBLENZ

The family all got together for supper on our daughter Verena's birthday Monday evening. It was quite a surprise on her to see them all come. We are a total of thirty-four when we all get together. Verena made six big pizzas, which were plenty for all of us. With everyone bringing food along, we had a variety to choose from. The table was full. Summertime is a good time to prepare meals because meal-planning is so much easier in summer since we can cook vegetables, make salads, and so on.

*Although these are called Morning Maple Muffins, they are good any time of day. We use our own maple syrup to make these muffins.*

## MORNING MAPLE MUFFINS

**2 cups all-purpose flour**
**½ packed cup brown sugar**
**2 teaspoons baking powder**
**½ teaspoon salt**
**¾ cup milk**
**½ cup (1 stick) butter, melted**
**½ cup maple syrup**
**¼ cup sour cream**
**1 egg, beaten**
**½ teaspoon vanilla extract**

**Topping**
**3 tablespoons all-purpose flour**
**3 tablespoons granulated sugar**
**2 tablespoons chopped nuts**
**½ teaspoon ground cinnamon**
**2 tablespoons cold butter**

In a large bowl, combine flour, brown sugar, baking powder, and salt. In another bowl, combine milk, butter, maple syrup, sour cream, egg, and vanilla. Stir milk mixture into flour mixture just until moistened. Fill greased or paper-lined muffin cups two-thirds full.

Prepare topping: Combine flour, sugar, nuts, and cinnamon; cut in butter until crumbly. Sprinkle over batter.

Bake at 400°F for 16–20 minutes. Cool 5 minutes before placing muffins on wire rack.

## AUGUST 2008

I need to make some pickles out of the many cucumbers I am getting right now. I'll probably make freezer pickles, and then I will put some of the other pickles in jars and make dill pickles. Also, red beets are being canned too. I don't really need more canned beets, as I have plenty now, but I will can whatever I have left. The children love red beets and will eat them for a snack. We always serve them with the church lunches too.

Church services were held at our neighbors' yesterday, followed by a noon lunch. We were also invited back for supper and for the youth singing. Our supper menu was "campfire stew" made in a kettle over the open fire. It was delicious, especially with all of the fresh vegetables in it. Also on the menu was coleslaw salad, egg salad, peanut butter, homemade pickles, homemade wheat and white bread, Jell-O, various kinds of pies, cake, and ice cream. Volleyball games and singing were done by the youth while parents visited with one an- other and watched the youth. It was a nice evening of fellowship, and it was relaxing to hear the youth all sing together.

*We usually buy a few bushels of peaches when they are harvested in the late summer or early fall. We can some and freeze some. When I freeze peaches I do some in small individual containers to pack in lunches. They keep the lunch cold and are a refreshing addition to a packed lunch.*

## PEACH BREAD

**1 (16-ounce) can sliced peaches, or 2 cups fresh, drained (reserve ¼ cup liquid)**
**2 cups flour**
**2 teaspoons baking powder**
**½ teaspoon salt**
**¼ cup chopped nuts**
**6 tablespoons butter**
**¾ packed cup brown sugar**
**2 eggs**

Finely chop or grate the peaches. In one bowl, combine the flour, baking powder, salt, and nuts. In another bowl, cream together the butter and brown sugar. Add the eggs and reserved ¼ cup peach liquid and mix well. Add the flour mixture and mix until well combined. Stir in the peaches.

Pour into two well-greased mini loaf pans and bake at 350°F for 40–45 minutes, or until a toothpick inserted in center comes out clean. Let cool in pans 10 minutes before turning out onto wire rack.

*Cinnamon rolls don't last long in our house. When they are almost finished baking and the smell starts wafting through the house, I suddenly get a lot of company in the kitchen! The pumpkin, along with the caramel frosting in this recipe, makes a tasty combination.*

## PUMPKIN CINNAMON ROLLS

⅔ cup milk

4 tablespoons butter plus additional to spread, softened

1 cup pumpkin puree

2 eggs, beaten

4 tablespoons granulated sugar

1 teaspoon salt

4½ teaspoons (2 packages) active dry yeast

4 cups flour plus additional for rolling

1 packed cup brown sugar

2 tablespoons ground cinnamon

Caramel cinnamon roll frosting (see below)

Heat milk and 4 tablespoons butter until butter is melted. Making sure mixture isn't too hot for the yeast, stir in pumpkin, eggs, granulated sugar, salt, yeast, and some of the flour. Mix well and add the remaining flour, mixing thoroughly. Cover and set in a warm place until doubled in size, about 1 hour.

Punch dough down and turn out onto floured surface. Sprinkle with enough flour to make dough easy to handle. Roll dough to about ¼ inch thick and spread with butter. Sprinkle with brown sugar and cinnamon. Roll up, cut into slices, and place on a greased 10 x 15-inch jelly-roll pan. Let rise until doubled in size. Bake at 350°F for 20 minutes. Cool, then frost with caramel frosting (see page 56).

## CARAMEL CINNAMON ROLL FROSTING

**½ cup (1 stick) butter**
**1 packed cup brown sugar**
**¼ cup evaporated milk or cream**
**2 cups confectioners' sugar**

Melt butter in a saucepan; add brown sugar. Boil over low heat about 2 minutes, stirring constantly. Add evaporated milk; continue stirring until mixture comes to a full boil. Remove from heat and let cool. Add confectioners' sugar, beating well, until frosting is the right consistency.

*Zucchini bread is always good with any meal. We mostly make this in the spring and summer months when we have our own zucchini from the garden. You can shred and freeze zucchini when you have abundance, measuring two cups into each freezer pack. Make sure to drain it well when you are ready to use it.*

## ZUCCHINI BREAD

3 eggs
1 cup vegetable oil
2 cups granulated sugar
2 cups peeled and grated zucchini
3 teaspoons vanilla extract
3 cups all-purpose flour
3 teaspoons ground cinnamon
1 teaspoon baking soda
1 teaspoon baking powder
1 teaspoon salt
1 cup chopped nuts

In a bowl, beat the eggs until foamy; add the oil, sugar, zucchini, and vanilla. Mix lightly, but thoroughly. Mix in the flour, cinnamon, baking soda, baking powder, and salt. Stir in nuts. Divide the batter between two greased 9 x 5-inch loaf pans. Bake at 325°F for 1 hour, or until a toothpick inserted in the center comes out clean.

*This recipe is easy if you just want to make one loaf of bread. Our children like homemade bread for grilled cheese sandwiches.*

## WHITE BREAD

**1 cup very warm water**
**1 teaspoon canola oil**
**1 scant teaspoon salt**
**1 tablespoon granulated sugar**
**1 teaspoon active dry yeast**
**3 cups bread flour**

Combine water, oil, salt, sugar, and yeast in order given. Let stand until yeast dissolves. Stir in half the flour; beat until smooth. Add remaining flour and knead by hand. If dough sticks to your hands, grease them lightly. Cover dough and let stand in a warm place to rise until doubled in size.

Knead lightly and let rise again until doubled. Punch down and put dough in a greased 9 x 5-inch loaf pan. Prick the top in a few places to release air bubbles. Let rise until doubled in size. Bake at 350°F for 30 minutes, or until golden brown. Rub butter on top of loaf after removing from oven. Remove from pan and let cool.

**My daughter** Susan always helped me make bread, but she never did it herself until after she was married. "Mose loves his homemade bread, so I make bread," she says. My daughter Elizabeth's husband, Tim, thinks store-bought bread is a treat because his mom always made her own bread.

Soups &
Sandwiches

*I still remember when my mother would soak beans. Beans were served often, in different recipes, when I was a child, probably because it was an inexpensive way to feed our large family. My mom always made them taste good no matter how she prepared them.*

## BACON BEAN SOUP

**1 pound dried Great Northern beans, soaked overnight**

**4 cups chicken stock plus more as needed**

**4 cups water**

**1 pound bacon, cut into 1-inch pieces**

**1 onion, diced**

**2 stalks celery, diced**

**2 carrots, peeled and diced**

**Salt and pepper**

**4 cloves garlic, minced**

**Fresh parsley, minced (about ⅛ cup)**

Rinse beans and put into a large pot, then add chicken stock and water. Bring to a boil, then reduce to a simmer.

While the beans are cooking, fry the bacon in a large skillet over medium heat until barely crisp. Drain on a paper towel-lined plate. Add bacon to the simmering beans. Drain most of the bacon drippings from the skillet and add the onion, celery, and carrots. Season with salt and pepper as desired, and cook until vegetables just begin to soften. Add garlic and cook another 1–2 minutes. Add the vegetables to the beans. Then add parsley.

Cover and cook on low until beans are tender, about 1½ hours. If the liquid gets too low, add an additional 1 cup chicken stock.

*My grandmother always made tomato soup, and then my mother did too. I never cared much for the taste of it, so I don't make it too often for my family. My daughter Susan says her husband, Mose, likes to eat this soup over toast.*

# TOMATO SOUP

**2 cups tomato juice**
**1 cup crushed tomatoes**
**1 teaspoon baking soda**
**1 quart (4 cups) milk**
**2 tablespoons butter**
**Salt and pepper**

Combine tomato juice and tomatoes in a saucepan; heat to boiling. Once boiling, turn heat to low and add baking soda while stirring (it will foam). When foam subsides, add the milk and cook until heated through, but do not boil. Once heated, add butter and season with salt and pepper to taste.

## JANUARY 1999, ELIZABETH COBLENZ

My mother didn't have to use a cookbook for her cooking. We had all kinds of soups when we were smaller. There were soups like bean soup, rivvel soup, potato soup, vegetable soup, brown flour soup, coffee soup, beef and homemade noodle soup, and a potpie soup. Mother didn't have recipes for any of these, she just knew how much of this and that to put in.

When you think to back then, meals were much simpler and probably better for our health. In the summer months when it was hot, a cold milk soup was on the menu for supper. Sweetened cold milk was poured over crumbled bread, strawberries, mulberries, raspberries, or bananas. We could change the cold soup as different fruit came in and out of season.

*I love to make this soup in the fall when we have fresh cabbage from our garden. The cooler evenings signal the change of season and let us know summer is coming to an end.*

## HAM AND CABBAGE SOUP

**2 tablespoons butter**
**¼ cup minced onion**
**¼ cup chopped celery**
**¼ cup flour**
**½ teaspoon salt**
**⅛ teaspoon black pepper**
**3 cups water**
**2 cups chopped or shredded cabbage**
**2 cups diced cooked ham**
**¾ cup sour cream**

Melt butter in a large pan; then sauté onion and celery until tender. Add flour, salt, and pepper, blending until smooth. Add water and cook until mixture comes to a boil, stirring constantly. Add cabbage; cover and simmer until cabbage is tender, about 10 minutes. Stir in ham and cook until heated through. Blend in sour cream. Heat through, but do not boil.

*Having our own ground beef in the freezer to use makes this an easy meal, especially when the garden has potatoes and carrots ready for harvesting.*

## HEARTY HAMBURGER SOUP

**1 pound ground beef**

**2 tablespoons butter**

**1 cup sliced carrots**

**1 cup chopped onion**

**1 cup peeled and diced potatoes**

**2 cups tomato juice**

**1½ teaspoons salt**

**⅓ cup flour**

**4 cups milk**

In a skillet, brown the ground beef. When the meat is cooked through, drain the drippings. In a large pot, melt butter. Add carrots, onion, and potatoes and cook until tender. Add tomato juice, salt, and cooked ground beef, and cook over medium heat until almost boiling. Stir the flour into the milk until combined, then add to the soup. Simmer until heated through.

*I always like having vegetable soup canned in jars sitting on the shelves in my canning room in the basement. It makes a quick lunch or an easy side with a light supper. You can omit or add any vegetables you like.*

## VEGETABLE SOUP (*to can or freeze*)

**1 pound ground beef**
**1 quart (4 cups) peeled and diced carrots**
**1 quart (4 cups) peeled and diced potatoes**
**½ quart (2 cups) chopped celery**
**½ quart (2 cups) chopped onion**
**1 quart (4 cups) peas**
**1 quart (4 cups) corn**
**2 cups uncooked pasta noodles (any kind, but I prefer smaller-sized pasta)**
**1 (16-ounce) can cannellini beans, drained and rinsed**
**6 quarts (1½ gallons) tomato juice**
**Chili powder**
**Salt and pepper**

Brown ground beef in a skillet and drain the drippings. In a large stock-pot, combine all ingredients, adding chili powder and salt and pepper as desired, and simmer until vegetables are tender, about 1 hour. It will take a while to get the large pot to the simmer stage. Follow USDA guidelines for canning or freezing.

Makes 12 quarts.

**My mom** always made vegetable soup when all my sisters and I and our children came over. My children started calling it "Grandma Soup," and she'd often make it when we visited. She used home-canned beef chunks, potatoes, carrots, peas, beans, and beef stock. She always got the seasonings just right. Now I'll make a big batch of "Grandma Soup" and can it, and put some of it in Joe's thermos for lunch.

*We had this soup quite often when I was growing up, using milk from our cows, which made for a creamier soup. My mom didn't have bags of frozen mixed vegetables like those we can buy today, so she used her own canned vegetables.*

## MOM'S CHEESE SOUP

**¼ cup (½ stick) butter**

**¼ cup minced onion**

**¼ cup flour**

**4 cups milk**

**Salt**

**1 cup shredded cheddar cheese**

**1 (10-ounce) package frozen mixed vegetables, cooked according to package directions**

Melt butter in saucepan. Add onions, and sauté until onions are clear. Blend in flour, milk, and salt to taste. Cook until thick, stirring constantly. Add cheese and stir until melted. Add cooked vegetables and simmer until heated through.

**One of my girls'** favorites is one-kettle soup, made with potatoes, beef chunks, spaghetti noodles, salt, pepper, and water. It's very soothing to the stomach. Daughter Elizabeth makes one-kettle soup for dinner sometimes, which her husband, Tim, never had growing up.

## OCTOBER 2002

This weekend was the second time for butchering chickens during the past month. On Labor Day we butchered ten chickens and four roosters. Mom had been here to show us how to clean and butcher them. I am glad she could show us yet. Mom came the next day and helped me to process twenty-one quarts of chicken. Joe grilled the four young roosters that evening. Our daughter Elizabeth brought home some little chickens from school last spring. Those four roosters were among them. Elizabeth had fun feeding and watering them, and watching them grow.

I remember when I was younger that Dad and Mom butchered chickens. I was the third youngest of us children and was too young to help. I was always amazed at how the chickens could still jump around after their heads had been chopped off. We have twelve chickens left, and the children enjoy gathering the eggs. Joe and the children love homemade chicken noodle soup. The homegrown chickens make the best broth.

*We like potatoes, so I enjoy fixing them in different ways. My husband, Joe, likes potato soup with a lot of vegetables along with the potatoes, because then the soup has much more flavor.*

## POTATO ONION CHEESE SOUP

**2 tablespoons vegetable or olive oil**

**1 large clove garlic, minced**

**1–2 large onions, chopped**

**2 stalks celery, cut fine**

**½ green bell pepper, chopped**

**2 large carrots, thinly sliced**

**4 large potatoes, peeled and cubed**

**2 cups chicken broth**

**½ teaspoon salt**

**½ teaspoon black pepper**

**1 cup milk**

**⅓ cup (about 5 tablespoons) butter**

**⅓ cup sour cream**

**2 cups shredded cheddar cheese (8 ounces)**

Pour oil into a large pot and sauté the garlic, onions, celery, bell pepper, and carrots over medium heat for 10 minutes. Add the potatoes, chicken broth, salt, and pepper, and simmer for an additional 20 minutes, or until potatoes are tender.

Stir in milk, butter, and sour cream and simmer a few more minutes, but do not boil. Sprinkle each individual serving with cheese.

*My son-in-law Mose, married to Susan, often makes sloppy joes. He doesn't have a recipe, so I watched him make it one time, and now I try to make it the way he does. The venison helps "dry up" the sausage so it's not so wet for sandwiches. Sometimes we don't even use hamburger buns when we serve this dish.*

## SLOPPY JOES

**1 pound pork sausage**
**1 pound ground venison**
**¼ firmly packed cup brown sugar**
**2 tablespoons maple syrup**
**1 tablespoon Worcestershire sauce**
**¼ cup barbecue sauce**
**½ cup ketchup**
**1 tablespoon prepared mustard**
**1 teaspoon onion salt or powder**
**½ teaspoon garlic salt or powder**
**Hamburger buns**

In a skillet or large pan, brown sausage and venison. Drain drippings. Stir in remaining ingredients and simmer for 15–30 minutes over low heat so flavors come together. Stir occasionally as mixture simmers. Serve on buns.

*We make our own pizza sauce, and it tastes delicious in this recipe. We butcher beef every winter, so we always have plenty of ground beef. You may also use venison.*

## PIZZA BURGERS

**2 pounds ground beef**
**1 pound ground bologna**
**¼ pound pepperoni**
**1 pound Velveeta cheese, cut into small cubes**
**2 cups pizza sauce**
**1 tablespoon sugar**
**1 tablespoon garlic powder**
**1½ teaspoons black pepper**
**12 hamburger buns**

Brown ground beef, drain, and allow to cool. In a large bowl, combine bologna with pepperoni and cheese and add cooled beef. Mix in pizza sauce, sugar, garlic powder, and pepper.

Place hamburger bun halves on a baking sheet. Spread mixture over buns and bake at 350°F for 15 minutes.

Makes 24 open-faced sandwiches.

**When we butcher** a cow, we keep everything that we can, including the brain, tongue, heart, and liver. We fry the brain and it looks like a fried chicken breast when it's done. My husband Joe likes it served for breakfast with eggs and potatoes.

*My family likes ham and cheese sandwiches for breakfast sometimes, especially when we have somewhere we need to be early in the day and don't have time for a big breakfast.*

## HAM AND CHEESE STICKY BUNS

**1 dozen dinner rolls**
**24 thin slices deli ham**
**24 thin slices deli turkey**
**12 slices provolone cheese**

**Sauce**
**½ cup (1 stick) butter**
**1 tablespoon Worcestershire sauce**
**2 tablespoons brown sugar**
**1 tablespoon poppy seeds**
**1 tablespoon dry mustard**
**½ teaspoon onion powder**
**¼ teaspoon garlic powder**

Make sandwiches, dividing ham, turkey, and cheese evenly between the rolls. Place on a baking sheet.

Prepare sauce: Heat sauce ingredients together until butter and brown sugar are melted, mixing well. Drizzle over sandwiches. Refrigerate 6 hours or overnight. Bake, uncovered, at 350°F for 10 minutes. Cover loosely with foil and bake another 10 minutes.

# Meats & Main Dishes

*I enjoy making a meal like this when we are home on a Sunday because when the ribs are in the oven, there is nothing more I need to do until they are done. I set the oven timer, clean up the dishes, and read or play a game while the ribs bake. I prefer Johnny's seasoning salt in this recipe.*

## BAKED BARBECUE RIBS

**1 tablespoon shortening**

**3–5 pounds country-style ribs**

**Salt and pepper**

**Seasoned salt**

**3–4 large white onions, cut into chunks**

**2 cloves garlic, minced**

**2 cups ketchup**

**½ packed cup brown sugar**

**1 tablespoon prepared yellow mustard**

**1 tablespoon Worcestershire sauce**

**2 tablespoons white vinegar**

Melt shortening in a sauté pan and sear the ribs on each side. Place in a 9 x 13-inch baking dish. Sprinkle with salt and pepper and seasoned salt as desired. Sprinkle onions over the ribs.

In a small bowl, mix together garlic, ketchup, brown sugar, mustard, Worcestershire sauce, and vinegar. Pour over ribs and onions. Bake, covered, at 325°F for 1½ hours, then uncover and bake an additional 1½ hours. Baste as needed.

*This is an easy way to make a spaghetti meal. Sometimes I cut the bacon in little pieces instead of laying them in strips across the top. If I have fried bacon left over from another meal, I mix it up right into the spaghetti.*

## BAKED SPAGHETTI CASSEROLE

**1 pound ground beef**
**1 cup chopped celery**
**½ cup chopped onion**
**8 ounces spaghetti noodles**
**1 cup shredded mozzarella cheese**
**1 quart (4 cups) tomato juice, or enough to moisten**
**1 tablespoon sugar**
**4 strips uncooked bacon**
**Salt and pepper**

Brown ground beef, celery, and onion in a skillet; drain drippings. Cook spaghetti in water as directed; drain, then mix in cheese, tomato juice, and sugar. Combine meat mixture and spaghetti. Put into a 9 x 13-inch baking dish. Top with bacon strips. Season with salt and pepper as desired. Bake at 400°F for 30 minutes, or until bacon is fully cooked.

### AUGUST 1992, ELIZABETH COBLENZ

Gardens are plentiful! We are filling those empty jars now for those long winter months ahead to feed family. We will can green beans, peas, sweet corn, red beets, and pickles. It seems our work is endless and the hours are too short to get everything done. But I guess we should appreciate our good health to do it.

*Growing up, I disliked cabbage or anything made from cabbage. I think as we grow older our taste buds learn to like more foods, because now cabbage is a vegetable I really enjoy.*

## CABBAGE ROLLS

**1 head cabbage**
**1 tablespoon plus 1 teaspoon salt**
**½ pound ground beef**
**1 onion, minced**
**1 cup cooked rice**
**½ teaspoon chopped garlic**
**¼ teaspoon paprika**
**¼ teaspoon black pepper**
**4 cups tomato juice**
**2–4 cups sauerkraut**

Put whole cabbage in a large pot of boiling water, add 1 tablespoon salt, and boil for 5 minutes until tender. Carefully remove cabbage, drain, cool, and separate leaves.

Brown ground beef and onion in a skillet, drain, and add cooked rice, garlic powder, paprika, pepper, and remaining 1 teaspoon salt. Place ¼ cup filling in each cabbage leaf, roll, and secure with toothpicks. Place in a greased 9 x 13-inch baking dish. Pour tomato juice over the rolls. Add a layer of sauerkraut. Bake at 350°F for 45–60 minutes.

*When I have fresh tomatoes from the garden, I use those instead of the tomato juice. I peel them and cook them down, then put the tomato chunks and juice all in.*

---

# GOOD GOULASH

**1 pound ground beef**
**½ onion, chopped**
**2 cups macaroni noodles**
**1 quart (4 cups) tomato juice**
**2 cups marinara sauce**
**¼ cup granulated sugar**
**¾ teaspoon salt**
**¾ teaspoon chili powder**
**Hot mashed potatoes, for serving**

Brown ground beef and onion together in a skillet. Drain. Boil macaroni noodles for 10 minutes; drain. Combine all ingredients, except for potatoes, in a saucepan and simmer for 15–20 minutes. Serve over mashed potatoes.

### SEPTEMBER 1999, ELIZABETH COBLENZ

We're canning tomato juice together today. We keep canning tomatoes as to not leave them go to waste. It's so good to fill jars for the long winter ahead. I'm so glad when the children fill their jars for the winter, also. I think my jars are all full enough now, but I am sharing with the children what is from my garden. It just doesn't take as much for us anymore since there are not so many at the table, although the children and their families still come home for meals, which we so enjoy.

*We love chicken wings. Some in our family, including the little grandchildren, eat the wings without the sauce. I like to eat my wings with hot sauce, and others like their wings with barbecue sauce. Most times we cook them on a charcoal grill.*

## CHICKEN HOT WINGS

**3 pounds chicken wings**
**4 cloves garlic, minced**
**1 tablespoon grated fresh ginger**
**½ cup soy sauce**
**2 tablespoons freshly squeezed lime juice**
**2 tablespoons olive oil**
**1 teaspoon hot red pepper flakes**
**¼ teaspoon ground cinnamon**
**Hot sauce of your choice**

Separate wings at the joints and discard the skinny tips (or use them to make chicken broth). Combine all ingredients, including hot sauce as desired, in a large resealable plastic bag and refrigerate several hours. Discard the marinade. Place wings in a baking dish and bake at 375°F until they are cooked through, about 30 minutes. The wings may be grilled, if preferred.

## LOVINA'S DAUGHTER ELIZABETH

One time I tried to make chicken potpie, but it was a disaster. We sat down to eat, and my husband, Tim, was eating it. I took a taste but could hardly stand it. I asked Tim how he could eat it; he said he didn't want to make me feel bad. I had two pizzas in the freezer, so we ate those instead. Now I always have frozen pizzas on hand just in case.

*This recipe makes for a good hearty meal anytime, but it is especially welcome on a chilly winter evening. When Joe or the children return from doing the evening chores of caring for the animals and come in to the smell of this potpie in the oven, they can't wait for me to get the dinner on the table. The hot meal quickly warms them up!*

## CHICKEN POTPIE

**1 cup cubed boneless chicken**

**1 cup peeled and sliced potatoes**

**½ cup peeled and sliced carrots**

**½ cup chopped celery**

**½ cup chopped onion**

**½ cup (1 stick) butter**

**½ cup flour**

**½ teaspoon garlic salt**

**½ teaspoon black pepper**

**1¾ cups chicken broth, or 1 cube chicken bouillon or 1 teaspoon chicken soup base dissolved in 1¾ cups reserved cooking water**

**⅔ cup milk**

**1 (9-inch) crust for a two-crust, deep-dish pie**

**1 egg**

**1 tablespoon water**

In saucepan, combine chicken, potatoes, carrots, and celery. Add water to cover, bring to a boil, and boil for 15 minutes. Remove from heat and drain, reserving 1¾ cups liquid if you don't plan to use chicken broth. Dissolve bouillon or soup base in the liquid and set aside.

In the saucepan over medium heat, sauté the onion in butter. Stir in flour, garlic salt, and pepper. Slowly stir in the chicken broth (or reserved cooking liquid) and milk. Simmer over medium heat until thick. Remove from heat and set aside.

Roll out half the pie crust and place in a deep-dish pie pan. Place chicken mixture in crust, then pour hot liquid over it. Roll out remaining crust and use to cover pie. Seal edges, then make about six slits in top crust. Make an egg wash by beating together egg and water. Brush the egg wash on the crust with a pastry brush. Bake at 425°F for 30–35 minutes, or until crust is golden brown. Let stand 10 minutes before serving.

*Our children don't really care so much for green beans when I cook them plain, but when I put them in soup or a casserole, they don't mind them with the other flavors.*

## GREEN BEAN CASSEROLE

**1 pound ground beef**
**1 small onion, chopped**
**8 ounces egg noodles**
**1 quart (4 cups) canned green beans or fresh green beans, cooked**
**2 cups grated cheese**

Brown ground beef and onion in a skillet. Cook noodles according to package instructions; drain. Add noodles to meat and stir in green beans. Grease a baking dish and pour in mixture. Top with cheese and bake at 350°F for 30–40 minutes.

*Some years we raise chickens just for meat. They are a different type of chicken from our layers (chickens which we keep to lay eggs), and are called broilers. I like to use cut-up chicken breasts for casseroles like this one.*

## OVERNIGHT CHICKEN CASSEROLE

**2 cups cooked and chopped chicken**

**8 ounces spaghetti noodles, cooked**

**½ pound cheese, grated**

**4 hard-cooked eggs, diced**

**1 small onion, minced**

**2 cups milk**

**2 (10½-ounce) cans cream of mushroom soup (do not dilute)**

Thoroughly mix together all ingredients and place in a greased 9 x 13-inch baking pan. Cover and refrigerate overnight. Remove from refrigerator 1 hour before putting in the oven. Bake, uncovered, at 350°F for 1 hour.

### LOVINA'S DAUGHTER ELIZABETH

During our first year as a married couple I would make meals using recipes I had gotten from my mom, but we ended up with so much extra that I had to cut the recipes in half. One of the first things I made was tater tot casserole; in fact, that was what I made when everyone came to my house for the first time after Tim and I got married.

*If you like stir-fry, this is a great combination of pork and vegetables. If you like a little more meat, you can increase the amount of pork. I have also used fresh beef or chicken instead of the pork.*

## PORK 'N' PEPPER STIR-FRY

1 cup cubed pork

3 tablespoons vegetable oil

1½ cups celery cut into julienne strips or bite-sized pieces

1 medium green or red bell pepper, cut into julienne strips or bite-sized pieces

1 medium onion, cut into small wedges

1 clove garlic, minced

2 tablespoons cornstarch

1¼ cups cold water

2 tablespoons soy sauce

¼ teaspoon salt

Hot cooked rice, for serving

In a skillet, cook pork in oil until tender. Remove from pan and set aside. Sauté celery, bell pepper, onion, and garlic in remaining oil until crisp-tender. Combine cornstarch and water, stirring until smooth; stir into vegetables. Return pork to skillet and add soy sauce and salt. Bring to a boil and cook, stirring, for 2 minutes, or until thickened. Serve over rice.

### APRIL 1999, ELIZABETH COBLENZ

Well, I made a one-kettle soup of beef chunks, noodles, diced potatoes, one onion, and salt and pepper to taste. Plus, rare beef was on the menu. Do you all know what rare beef is? Beef is sliced thin. Then lard is put into a skillet until it is good and hot. Then, slice by slice, we put well-seasoned, with salt and pepper, beef slices into that lard. We just stir a couple of rounds on both sides and then take it out. I can recall that my dad would really have it peppered down.

*This chicken has a good flavor. The molasses and brown mustard make a tasty dish.*

## SWEET AND SPICY BAKED CHICKEN

**4 pounds bone-in chicken pieces with skin**
**Salt and pepper**
**⅔ cup molasses**
**⅓ cup spicy brown mustard**

Season chicken with salt and pepper as desired. Arrange in a single layer in a glass baking dish or cast iron pan. Bake 20 minutes at 450°F. Meanwhile, mix molasses and mustard in a bowl. Skim off fat from the baking dish and pour two-thirds of the molasses mixture over chicken to coat, reserving the remaining sauce. Bake an additional 25 minutes for breasts or 35 minutes for thighs, basting every 5 minutes with the sauce in the pan. Serve with remaining sauce.

**My sister** Susan is the youngest of my dad and mom's eight children. As a child, she loved the skin from fried chicken and would save it to eat last. One day when she was young, she was playing with her nephew Ben in the playhouse. Leah, our oldest sister, came out to check on her son, who said, "She ate my skin!" Susan remembers this even years later.

*Round steak is a little tougher cut of meat, and cooking it longer will make it tender. Since we always have some in the freezer from our winter butchering, I look for recipes that have good flavors and longer cooking times.*

## SWISS STEAK

¼ cup all-purpose flour
1 teaspoon salt
¼ teaspoon black pepper
1½–2 pounds round steak, trimmed
2 tablespoons vegetable oil
1 cup chopped celery
1 cup chopped onion
8 ounces fresh mushrooms, sliced
1 clove garlic, minced
1 cup water
1 tablespoon steak sauce

Combine flour, salt, and pepper. Cut steak into serving-sized pieces; dredge in flour mixture. Heat oil in a skillet and brown the steak. Drain; place steak in a greased 2½-quart baking dish. Top with celery, onion, and mushrooms. Combine garlic, water, and steak sauce; pour over steak and vegetables. Cover and bake at 350°F for 1½ hours, or until the meat is tender.

Makes 6 servings.

*This is a good recipe to make after Thanksgiving when you have leftover turkey.*

## TURKEY HASH

**3 medium baking potatoes, peeled and quartered**
**1 teaspoon salt**
**6 slices bacon**
**1 onion, chopped**
**1½ pounds cooked turkey, finely chopped (about 3 cups)**
**½ teaspoon black pepper**
**Hot red pepper flakes**
**2 cups milk or turkey broth**
**5 tablespoons all-purpose flour**

Place potatoes in a medium saucepan with enough water to cover. Add salt, cover, and bring to a boil over high heat. Lower heat to a simmer and cook until the potatoes are barely tender, about 15 minutes. Drain and set aside.

Meanwhile, place bacon in a wide, deep saucepan, such as a Dutch oven. Cook over medium-low heat until bacon is crisp. Remove from pan and set aside. Add onion to bacon drippings in pan. Cook 5 minutes, stirring. Cut cooked potatoes into small cubes (less than ½ inch) and add to onion. Add cooked turkey, black pepper, and red pepper flakes as desired.

Combine milk (or broth) and flour in a jar with a tight-fitting lid and shake vigorously to combine. Pour all at once into pan with turkey. Increase heat to high and bring to a boil, stirring constantly. When the mixture thickens, taste and adjust seasonings as desired.

Pour into a serving bowl and crumble bacon over the top. Serve over corn waffles, biscuits, toast, or toasted English muffins.

Leftovers can be thinned with milk or broth and served hot as turkey chowder.

*This is a good recipe when zucchini are plentiful. We eat zucchini a lot of different ways, and this is a tasty one-dish meal!*

## ZUCCHINI PIZZA CASSEROLE

**4 cups shredded zucchini (do not peel)**
**½ teaspoon salt**
**¼ teaspoon fajita seasoning**
**2 eggs, beaten**
**½ cup grated Parmesan cheese**
**1 cup shredded cheddar cheese, divided**
**2 cups shredded mozzarella cheese, divided**
**1 pound sausage or ground beef**
**½ cup chopped onion**
**2 cups pizza sauce, or 2 cups ketchup plus ¼ teaspoon dried oregano**
**1 green bell pepper, chopped**
**Mushrooms (optional)**

Place zucchini in strainer, sprinkle with salt and fajita seasoning. Drain for 10 minutes, then squeeze out moisture. Combine zucchini with eggs. Add Parmesan, ½ cup cheddar, and 1 cup mozzarella cheese. Press into a greased 9 x 13-inch baking pan. Bake at 400°F for 20 minutes.

Meanwhile, brown meat and onion in a skillet; drain. Add pizza sauce, bell pepper, and optional mushrooms. Spoon over baked zucchini mixture. Top with remaining ½ cup cheddar and 1 cup mozzarella cheese and bake for an additional 20 minutes, or until cheese is melted.

**One of my** daughter Susan's favorite dishes is pizza casserole. She always asked for it on her birthday—in fact, she'd eat it every day for a week if she could! She now makes her own home-made pizza sauce, but runs out of pizza sauce before the next season.

# Vegetables,
# Sides, *&*
# Salads

*This is a great way to use up those end-of-the-season vegetables from the garden. Until I started making this recipe, I had never bought balsamic vinegar. I skipped the fresh rosemary until my friend Ruth brought me rosemary to plant in my garden, and now I really enjoy using it in different dishes.*

## AUTUMN VEGETABLE DISH

**6 medium potatoes, cubed**

**2 sweet potatoes, peeled and cubed**

**2 medium onions, cut into 1-inch pieces**

**2 carrots, peeled and diced**

**1 butternut squash, peeled and cubed**

**1 red or green bell pepper, cut into 1-inch pieces**

**2 tablespoons balsamic vinegar**

**2 tablespoons olive oil**

**1 tablespoon chopped fresh thyme, or 1 teaspoon dried**

**1 tablespoon chopped fresh rosemary, or 1 teaspoon dried**

**1 teaspoon salt**

**½ teaspoon black pepper**

Arrange vegetables in a greased 9 x 13-inch baking dish. Mix the balsamic vinegar, oil, thyme, rosemary, salt, and pepper in a small bowl. Pour over vegetables and toss to coat. Bake at 425°F for 45 minutes, or until vegetables are tender. Stir once or twice while baking.

*We like to serve this dish with smoked sausage or roast chicken. I add boiled potatoes with butter to the menu to complete the meal.*

## BACON FRIED CABBAGE

**6 slices bacon, chopped**
**1 large onion, chopped**
**3 cloves garlic, minced**
**1 large head cabbage, cored and chopped**
**2 teaspoons seasoned salt**
**½ teaspoon black pepper**
**½ teaspoon onion powder**
**½ teaspoon garlic powder**

In a large pan, cook bacon until crisp; remove from pan, drain, and set aside. Discard all but 2 tablespoons of the bacon drippings. Use the drippings to cook the onion over medium heat until soft, about 4 minutes. Add garlic and cook for 1 minute. Stir in cabbage and cook 4–5 minutes. Add seasoned salt, pepper, onion powder, and garlic powder, stirring to combine.

Reduce heat to low; cover pan and simmer about 30 minutes, stirring occasionally. Just before serving, add reserved bacon.

*This is good served with mashed potatoes. When we make this gravy for weddings, we brown all the butter the day before to save time when cooking the day of the wedding.*

## BROWN BUTTER GRAVY

**1½ cups (3 sticks) butter**
**2¼ cups flour**
**2 quarts (8 cups) chicken stock**
**1 quart (4 cups) water**
**¼ cup chicken soup base**
**½ teaspoon salt**
**½ teaspoon black pepper**

Brown the butter: Heat butter in a skillet over medium heat. As the butter melts, it will begin to foam, and the color will change from yellow to tan to toasty brown. Remove from heat after it turns brown, being careful not to burn it. The butter will have a nutty aroma.

Add flour to the brown butter and stir until it becomes a paste. Set aside.

In a large skillet, heat chicken stock, water, soup base, salt, and pepper until warm. Add brown butter mixture, stirring with a wire whisk. Bring to a boil and boil a few minutes, stirring constantly.

**Weddings are a big event.** We've served mashed potatoes and gravy, noodles boiled in chicken broth, dressing, vegetables, and homemade dinner rolls or bread and cheese, and pies. At one of the weddings, we grilled six hundred pounds of chicken. We ordered the wedding wagon a year ahead, which has about 350 place settings and other dishes that we use in shifts. We rented coolers and freezers, and portable toilets for the one thousand guests. There are table waiters and coffee servers, with the younger girls serving as babysitters and the younger boys bringing water around.

*This can be used as a snack or as a side dish for a meal. You can use any vegetables you enjoy. I cut the vegetables pretty small so that each bar gets some of each vegetable on it.*

## VEGETABLE BARS

**Crust**

2 cups flour

1 tablespoon granulated sugar

1 teaspoon salt

1 teaspoon baking powder

½ cup shortening

¾ cup milk

**Filling layer**

1 (8-ounce) package cream cheese, softened

¾ cup sour cream

¾ cup mayonnaise

1 (1-ounce) package powdered ranch dressing mix (about 2 tablespoons)

**Toppings**

Green or red bell peppers

Cauliflower

Broccoli

Tomatoes

Onion

Carrots

2 cups shredded cheddar cheese (8 ounces)

6 slices bacon, fried and crumbled

For crust: Mix the crust ingredients and spread on a lightly greased 10 x 15-inch baking sheet. Bake at 400°F for 10 minutes, or until golden brown. Let cool.

For filling layer: In a medium bowl, combine all the filling ingredients and stir until well blended. Spread on cooled crust.

For toppings: Dice vegetables. Assemble over filling layer. Sprinkle cheese and bacon on top. Cover and refrigerate until ready to serve. Cut into small squares.

*I like to use sweet onions in this dish, but any onion will work. It is a good side for almost any meat, especially served with mashed potatoes.*

## CARROTS AND ONIONS

**1 pound carrots, sliced or coarsely shredded**
**1 cube chicken bouillon**
**1¼ cups water, divided**
**3 medium onions, chopped or sliced**
**¼ cup (½ stick) butter**
**1 tablespoon all-purpose flour**
**¼ teaspoon salt**
**Pepper**
**Granulated sugar**

In a medium pan, combine carrots and bouillon and ½ cup water (or enough to cover). Bring to a boil and simmer over medium heat for 10 minutes. In a separate pan, cook onions and butter until onions are transparent. Add flour, salt, and pepper, as desired, to onions, stir until blended, then add remaining ¾ cup water. When thickened, add carrots and sugar to taste. Simmer 10 minutes.

**When all us sisters** gathered at my mom's house, she would boil potatoes with the skins in a big pot. We'd make homemade sour cream (Miracle Whip, vinegar, milk, a little salt) and mash it all together. In the summer we'd also mash in lettuce or dandelion greens or endive. Sometimes we'd dice hard-cooked eggs with the dandelion greens and put that over the potatoes.

*I use a quart of my canned ground beef to make this gravy because it goes quicker not having to brown the meat. More flour or milk can be added to make more gravy. We like this served over mashed potatoes.*

## HAMBURGER GRAVY

**1 pound ground beef, or 1 quart canned**
**½ cup flour**
**1 teaspoon salt**
**1 teaspoon black pepper**
**1 cup milk**
**Toast, biscuits, or cooked potatoes, for serving**

If using fresh ground beef, brown in a skillet. Add flour, salt, and pepper, and continue browning. Add milk and simmer over medium heat, stirring constantly, until it is the consistency of gravy. Serve over toast, biscuits, or potatoes.

### FEBRUARY 1999, ELIZABETH COBLENZ

We got our pork and beef put up on Saturday. All our children and their families were here to help us, so it was a very enjoyable day of working together on our farm. Three quarters of beef were cut up, chunked, and put into jars. Beef was also ground into hamburger and put in jars to process. With the pork, we processed sausage, liver pudding, and pork chops. By the time we were done, we had everything in pints and quarts: 75 quarts of chunk beef, 39 quarts of hamburger, 53 quarts of sausage, 2 quarts of pork chops, and 23 quarts of liver pudding. We canned 180 quarts in all. Seven pressure cookers were in gear, so it made for a busy Saturday.

*When asparagus from our garden is in peak season, we have to come up with new ways to serve it. We like this recipe even without the toast or biscuits.*

## CREAMED HAM AND ASPARAGUS

**1 pound fresh asparagus, cut into 1-inch pieces**
**1½ cups milk, divided**
**1 tablespoon cornstarch**
**2 tablespoons butter**
**1 teaspoon salt**
**½ teaspoon black pepper**
**½ teaspoon dried parsley**
**1½ pounds cooked ham, cubed**
**3 hard-cooked eggs, chopped**
**2 cups shredded cheddar cheese (8 ounces)**
**Toast or biscuits, for serving**

In saucepan, cook asparagus in a small amount of water until tender. Drain and set aside.

Measure out 1½ cups milk in a liquid measuring cup. In medium saucepan, mix cornstarch with 2 tablespoons of the milk. Add butter, salt, pepper, and remaining milk. Cook over medium heat and stir until thickened.

Add dried parsley, ham, eggs, cheese, and asparagus; cook and stir over low heat until ham is warm and cheese is melted. Serve over toast or biscuits.

*The children like ranch dressing and anything ranch-flavored, so these potatoes disappear quickly when I make them with a meal.*

## RANCH POTATOES

**6–8 potatoes, peeled and cut into chunks**
**½ cup sour cream**
**1 cup ranch salad dressing**
**¼ cup cooked and crumbled bacon**
**2 tablespoons dried parsley**
**2 cups shredded cheddar cheese, divided**

Cook potatoes in salted water until tender. Drain and set aside.

Combine sour cream, ranch dressing, crumbled bacon, parsley, and 1 cup cheddar cheese. Toss gently with potatoes. Place in a greased 9 x 13-inch baking dish. Sprinkle with remaining 1 cup cheese. Bake, uncovered, at 350°F for 40–45 minutes.

### APRIL 2008

Our daughter Elizabeth, age thirteen, says dandelion greens taste too much like grass, although I don't think she has really ever tasted grass. Elizabeth and Susan went around the yard to pick the dandelions. They are very plentiful now, so it doesn't take too long to get enough for a meal. The girls don't like to wash them, though. We usually wash them quite a few times.

Sisters Susan and Verena told me that they tried dandelion salad with baked potatoes. They didn't think that tasted as good as with cooked potatoes. Our son Benjamin piped up and said, "Maybe the dog went potty on your dandelions and that is what tasted different." Benjamin is one who doesn't care for dandelions, and now I wonder if that is why.

*This recipe was given to me by my sister Susan. She made it and brought it here one Sunday when we were having a gathering. I like using lettuce fresh from my garden when I can.*

## LAYERED LETTUCE SALAD

1 head lettuce, chopped into bite-sized pieces
1 cup diced celery
4 hard-cooked eggs, diced
1 (10-ounce) package frozen peas
1 small sweet onion, diced
½ green bell pepper, diced
10 slices bacon, fried and diced
2 cups mayonnaise
2 tablespoons sugar
1 cup shredded cheddar cheese

Layer the first seven ingredients in a 9 x 13-inch dish, reserving some of the bacon to garnish the top. Mix the mayonnaise with the sugar and spread on top like a frosting. Top with cheese. Cover and refrigerate 8–12 hours. (The peas will thaw in the refrigerator.) At serving time, garnish with reserved bacon.

*This is a tasty salad! Although I do not care much for cooked sweet potatoes, I enjoy this salad. You can also use leftover baked sweet potatoes to make this dish.*

## SWEET POTATO SALAD

**2 pounds sweet potatoes**
**4 hard-cooked eggs, chopped**
**1½ cups finely chopped celery**
**8 green onions, sliced**
**1½ cups mayonnaise**
**2 teaspoons Dijon mustard**
**¼ teaspoon salt**

Peel and cube sweet potatoes. Place in pot with water just covering the potatoes, and boil 30–45 minutes, or until tender. Drain and cool. Add remaining ingredients, stir together, and refrigerate.

*I like to pick small zucchini from our garden for this dish. If your zucchini are big, chop them into smaller pieces instead of slicing them. This has different ingredients from your typical bean salad, and we enjoy the addition of the fresh vegetables.*

## ZUCCHINI BEAN SALAD

**3 small zucchini, thinly sliced**
**1½ cups chopped onion**
**¾ cup chopped green bell pepper**
**1 (16-ounce) can kidney beans, drained and rinsed**
**¼ cup vegetable oil**
**3 tablespoons vinegar**
**1 teaspoon garlic salt**
**¼ teaspoon black pepper**

In a medium bowl, combine zucchini, onion, bell pepper, and kidney beans. In a small bowl combine oil, vinegar, garlic salt, and pepper, stirring well. Pour over vegetable mixture. Refrigerate until ready to serve.

**One of the salads** my mom would make is called "overnight salad." She'd mix lettuce, cauliflower, peas, cheese, bacon, and sauce, and let it sit overnight to let the flavors blend.

*If your grocery store doesn't carry ditalini pasta, any small pasta would work, such as small shells. This makes a big batch and is great for taking to potluck dinners. This salad stays good for a few days.*

## COLESLAW PASTA SALAD

**1 (16-ounce) package ditalini pasta**
**1 (16-ounce) package coleslaw mix**
**1 sweet onion, finely chopped**
**2 stalks celery, finely chopped**
**2 medium cucumbers, seeded and finely chopped**
**1 green bell pepper, chopped**
**3 hard-cooked eggs, chopped**

**Dressing**
**½ cup mayonnaise**
**¼ cup cider vinegar**
**⅓ cup granulated sugar**
**½ teaspoon salt**
**¼ teaspoon black pepper**

Cook pasta according to package directions; drain and rinse in cold water. Place pasta in a large mixing bowl, then add coleslaw mix, onion, celery, cucumber, bell pepper, and eggs. Mix together.

Prepare dressing: In separate bowl, combine the dressing ingredients and stir with a wire whisk. Pour over the pasta salad and stir well to combine. Cover and refrigerate for 4–6 hours before serving.

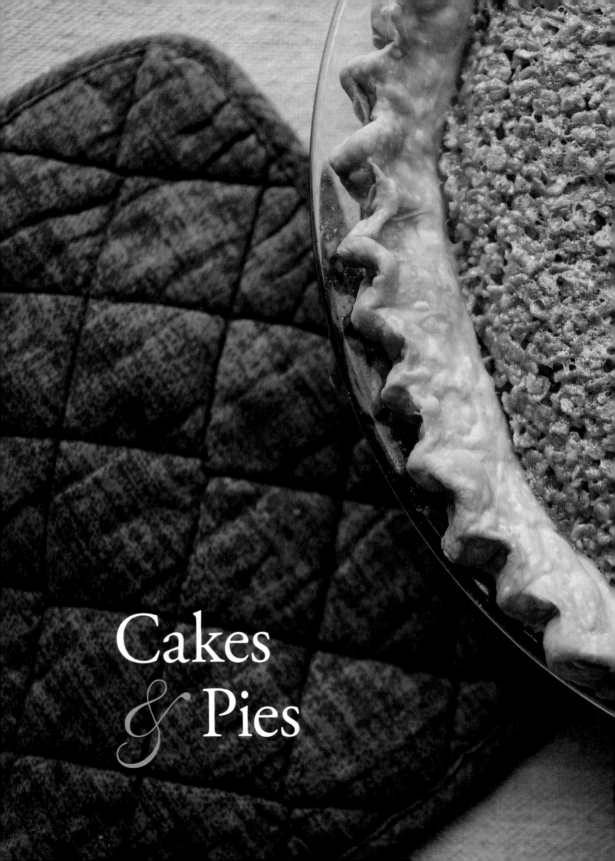

Cakes
& Pies

*This cake is good served with a little scoop of vanilla ice cream on the side. This cake can also be made in a 9 x 13-inch baking pan and baked longer, 35–40 minutes total, or until a toothpick inserted in the center comes out clean.*

## MAPLE SUGAR CAKE

½ cup (1 stick) butter, softened
1½ firmly packed cups brown sugar
3 eggs
½ cup maple syrup
½ cup milk
½ cup sour cream
1 teaspoon maple flavoring
2½ cups flour
1 teaspoon baking powder
1 teaspoon baking soda
½ teaspoon salt
½ teaspoon ground cloves
¼ teaspoon ground allspice
¼ teaspoon ground nutmeg
Maple sugar frosting (see next page)

In a large mixing bowl, cream together butter and brown sugar. Add eggs, one at a time, beating well after each addition. In a separate bowl, combine maple syrup, milk, sour cream, and maple flavoring. In another bowl, combine flour, baking powder, baking soda, salt, cloves, allspice, and nutmeg. Alternate adding flour mixture and syrup mixture to the butter and egg mixture. Stir gently to combine.

Pour batter into two greased and floured 9-inch round baking pans. Bake at 350°F for 20–25 minutes, or until a toothpick inserted in the centers comes out clean. Cool 10 minutes, then remove from pans and set on a wire rack to cool completely before frosting with maple sugar frosting.

## MAPLE SUGAR FROSTING

**6 tablespoons butter, softened**
**1½ teaspoons maple flavoring**
**4½ cups confectioners' sugar**
**½–¾ cup sour cream**
**1 cup chopped walnuts (optional)**

In a mixing bowl, cream together butter and maple flavoring. Gradually mix in confectioners' sugar. Add enough sour cream to achieve spreading consistency. Spread frosting between layers and over top and sides of cooled cake. Sprinkle with chopped walnuts if desired. Store in refrigerator.

### MAY 2009

I bought a horseshoe-shaped cake pan at a garage sale this spring. The children were eager to see how a cake would look shaped like a horseshoe, so daughter Elizabeth made one, frosted it, and edged it with chocolate chips, to take over to my sister Emma's. Needless to say, the children were all excited to see it and eat it. Quite a few of the children said they want a horseshoe cake for their birthdays this year! So it looks like here at the Eichers we will be having a lot of horseshoe-shaped cakes over the months ahead!

*We had a pear tree in our backyard when I was growing up. We ate the pears right from the tree, and Mom also canned pears for eating in the winter months. I like how moist the pears make this cake.*

## PEAR CAKE

**2 eggs**
**2 cups granulated sugar**
**1½ cups vegetable oil**
**3 cups flour**
**2 teaspoons ground cinnamon**
**1 teaspoon salt**
**1 teaspoon baking soda**
**1 teaspoon vanilla extract**
**1½ cups peeled and finely chopped fresh pear**

**Icing**
**1¼ cups confectioners' sugar**
**2 tablespoons milk**

In a large bowl, cream together eggs, sugar, and oil. Add flour, cinnamon, salt, baking soda, and vanilla; mix well. Stir in pears. Pour batter into a greased and floured tube pan (Bundt pan). Bake at 350°F for 60–65 minutes, or until a toothpick inserted in the center comes out clean. Let cool in pan 10 minutes before turning onto a plate.

To prepare icing, mix confectioners' sugar and milk together and drizzle over partially cooled cake.

**I remember** when my daughter Elizabeth was making her very first cake by herself when she was nine years old. She asked about the recipe calling for a whole egg. "Does that mean I have to put the shell in too?" she asked. I thought it was funny, but she sure didn't.

*This is a good moist cake with a lot of flavor. The crumbs in the center make it even better!*

## SUGAR CRUMB CAKE

**Batter**
3½ cups flour
2 cups granulated sugar
4 teaspoons baking powder
1 cup (2 sticks) butter
4 eggs
1½ cups milk
2 teaspoons vanilla extract

**Crumbs**
1 cup brown sugar
4 tablespoons flour
4 tablespoons butter, melted
1 teaspoon ground cinnamon
1 cup chopped nuts (optional)

To make batter, sift together flour, granulated sugar, and baking powder. Cut in butter with pastry blender or fork until mixture is fine. In a separate bowl, combine eggs, milk, and vanilla. Add half the egg mixture to the flour mixture and beat until smooth. Add remaining egg mixture and beat until smooth. Pour half the batter into a greased 9 x 13-inch baking pan.

To make crumbs, in another bowl, combine brown sugar, flour, melted butter, cinnamon, and optional chopped nuts. Use a fork to mix until crumbs form.

Sprinkle half the crumbs on top of the cake batter in the pan. Pour remaining batter on top. Sprinkle remaining crumbs on top.

Bake at 350°F for 45–55 minutes, or until a toothpick inserted in the center comes out clean.

---

**LOVINA'S DAUGHTER ELIZABETH**

My mom used to make us a birthday cake and would use whatever candy we had on hand, like gummy bears or Smarties, to spell out the name and age with the candy. Now I do that with my own kids.

*So often we have bananas that ripen before we get them eaten, so this is a good way to use them. This cake is light and tasty and makes a lot of servings.*

## FROSTED BANANA CAKE BARS

½ cup (1 stick) butter, softened

2 cups granulated sugar

3 large eggs

1½ cups mashed ripe banana (about 3 medium)

1 teaspoon vanilla extract

2 cups all-purpose flour

1 teaspoon baking soda

Dash salt

**Frosting**

1 (8-ounce) package cream cheese, softened

½ cup (1 stick) butter, softened

3 cups confectioners' sugar

2 teaspoons vanilla extract

½ cup finely chopped walnuts or pecans (optional)

In a large bowl, cream together butter and sugar until light and fluffy. Beat in the eggs, banana, and vanilla. Combine the flour, baking soda, and salt; stir into creamed mixture just until blended.

Transfer to a greased 10 x 15 x 1-inch baking pan. Bake at 350°F for 20–25 minutes, or until a toothpick inserted in the center comes out clean. Cool in pan on a wire rack.

To make frosting, beat together cream cheese and butter in a medium bowl until fluffy. Add confectioners' sugar and vanilla; beat until smooth. Frost cooled bars. Sprinkle walnuts or pecans over frosting, if desired.

*This is a simple recipe for making pie crust. It seems that once you find a pie crust that works well for you, that is the one you go to each time. This is a good go-to recipe.*

## PIE CRUST

**2 cups sifted all-purpose flour**
**1½ teaspoons salt**
**½ cup vegetable oil**
**¼ cup cold milk**

In a medium bowl, combine flour and salt. Pour oil and milk in small bowl and stir well. Add liquid mixture to flour and stir until mixed. Press into ball and divide in half. Place one half between two pieces of waxed paper and roll out in a circle to fit pie pan. Peel off top paper and place the crust in the pan paper side up and peel off the second paper. Gently fit crust into pan, then fill with pie filling. Trim off excess crust, leaving enough on edges to make a crimped crust edge. If making a double-crust pie, the second crust can be used for the top. Bake according to pie recipe.

To bake an unfilled pie shell, preheat the oven to 400°F. Place the pie shell in the freezer while the oven preheats. Line the chilled shell with aluminum foil or parchment paper, and fill it with pie weights or dried beans. Bake for 20 minutes. Remove from the oven and gently remove foil or parchment and the weights or beans. Return the pie shell to the oven for 10–20 more minutes, until golden brown all over. If the edges of the crust start to become too brown, cover them with a pie shield or strips of aluminum foil. Remove from the oven and cool completely before adding filling.

*Cherry pie is often served at weddings. We use a plastic lattice pie top cutter, which makes the look of a lattice on top but doesn't require the work of doing all the lattice crust by hand.*

## CHERRY PIE

**1 cup granulated sugar**
**3–4 tablespoons Clear Jel**
**Pinch salt**
**1 cup water**
**2 cups cherries, pitted**
**1 (9-inch) unbaked pie shell**

Make the filling the day before baking. Mix sugar and Clear Jel in a saucepan; add salt, then add water. Bring to a boil and cook 1 minute, then add cherries. Stir over medium heat for 1–2 minutes. Cool and refrigerate overnight.

When ready to bake, pour cherry mixture into unbaked pie shell. Bake at 375°F for 45–60 minutes.

**I never baked** a pie alone until I was married and away from home because my mom always did the breads and pies. She'd just tell us what to do; she never used measuring spoons or cups. When I'd ask how much lard to use, she'd say, "The size of an egg."

*If you like lemon pie you will love this recipe! I don't always use the lemon rind, and it still turns out good.*

## LEMON PIE

**3 tablespoons cornstarch**
**1¼ cups plus 6 tablespoons granulated sugar**
**1 tablespoon grated lemon rind**
**¼ cup lemon juice**
**3 eggs, separated**
**1½ cups boiling water**
**1 (9-inch) prebaked pie shell**

In a medium saucepan, combine cornstarch, 1¼ cups sugar, grated lemon rind, and lemon juice. Beat egg yolks, then add to cornstarch mixture. Slowly stir in boiling water, being careful not to cook the eggs. Over medium heat, bring mixture to a boil and cook on a slow boil for 4 minutes, stirring constantly. Pour into prebaked pie shell.

Beat eggs whites until stiff but not dry. Beat in remaining 6 tablespoons sugar a tablespoon at a time. Spread the meringue over top of pie, spreading to the edge to seal in the filling.

Bake at 425°F degrees for 4–5 minutes, or until meringue is browned. Cool on rack away from draft. Keep refrigerated until ready to serve.

### JULY 1993, ELIZABETH COBLENZ

The weather was ideal for the wedding of our daughter Lovina and Joe C. Eicher. The Tuesday before the wedding on Thursday, July 15, about two dozen women came to help. They baked ninety pies (oatmeal, cherry, raisin, and rhubarb) and made fourteen batches of nothings. On Wednesday about a dozen girls came to peel potatoes, cut up vegetables for the dressing, and made potato salad. I had cooked the potatoes in a twenty-quart cooker. The tables were set and the last-minute cleaning was done.

Then came the wedding day. We started to fry chicken (three hundred pounds) at four fifteen in the morning to have it ready for dinner. We also served boneless ham. The meals consisted of mashed potatoes, chicken and noodles, gravy, dressing, buttered corn, green beans (which came out of the garden), pork and beans, potato salad, carrot salad, lettuce salad (plenty from the garden), hot peppers, Swiss cheese, fruit salad, tapioca pudding, pies, cakes, nothings, celery sticks, coffee, bread, rhubarb jam, and butter!

*My mother made oatmeal pie a lot. She always said the older the pie gets, the better the taste. So if you need to bake a pie a few days ahead, this would be a good pie to make. My children think it tastes a lot like pecan pie without the pecans.*

## OATMEAL PIE

2 eggs, slightly beaten
¾ cup granulated sugar
¾ cup light corn syrup
¾ cup quick-cooking oats
¾ cup flaked coconut
¼ cup (½ stick) butter, melted
1 (9-inch) unbaked pie shell

In a medium bowl, stir together eggs, sugar, and corn syrup. Add oats, coconut, and butter, and mix well. Pour into unbaked pie shell. Bake at 350°F for 45–50 minutes. Let cool 15 minutes before serving. Good served with ice cream or whipped cream.

*Pumpkin pie is a favorite of ours. This pie is often served at weddings. When I grow my own pumpkins I like to can the pumpkin to use later in pies and bars.*

## PUMPKIN PIE

**1 egg**
**½ cup granulated sugar**
**1 cup pumpkin puree**
**1 cup milk**
**½ teaspoon vanilla extract**
**1 tablespoon all-purpose flour**
**1 teaspoon ground cinnamon**
**1 teaspoon pumpkin pie spice**
**1 (9-inch) unbaked pie shell**

In a large bowl, whisk egg until well beaten. Add sugar, pumpkin, milk, vanilla, flour, cinnamon, and pumpkin pie spice. Stir by hand or mix with a beater until well blended. Pour into unbaked pie shell. Bake at 425°F for 15 minutes, then reduce oven temperature to 350°F and bake for an additional 45–50 minutes, or until a knife inserted in center of pie comes out clean. Let cool; refrigerate until ready to serve. Can be served warm or cold.

*We buy apples by the bushel in the fall when they are plentiful. Many varieties stay a good long time through the fall and winter months. We store them in our enclosed back porch because it stays cool enough in there. I like to pick out the ones that get spots and use them in pie.*

## SOUR CREAM APPLE PIE

**2 eggs**
**1 cup sour cream (8 ounces)**
**1 cup granulated sugar**
**6 tablespoons all-purpose flour, divided**
**1 teaspoon vanilla extract**
**¼ teaspoon salt**
**3 cups peeled and chopped baking apples**
**1 (9-inch) unbaked pie shell**
**¼ cup brown sugar**
**3 tablespoons cold butter**

In a large bowl, whisk eggs. Add sour cream. Stir in granulated sugar, 2 tablespoons flour, vanilla, and salt; mix well. Stir in apples. Pour into unbaked pie shell. Bake at 375°F for 15 minutes.

Meanwhile, combine brown sugar and remaining 4 tablespoons flour, and cut in butter until mixture is crumbly. After pie has baked for 15 minutes, remove pie from the oven and sprinkle crumbs over the top. Bake for an additional 20–25 minutes, or until filling is set. Cool completely on wire rack. Serve, or cover and refrigerate.

*When my mother baked pies and she had an extra crust left, she would fill it with breadcrumbs and make this pie. She said she didn't think the pie was a good pie to take somewhere, and was just for us to eat at home. Even though the ingredients are quite simple it is a surprisingly tasty pie.*

## POOR MAN'S BREAD PIE

**1 (9-inch) unbaked pie shell**
**2–3 cups breadcrumbs (can be made from stale bread)**
**1 tablespoon flour**
**6 teaspoons granulated sugar**
**2 tablespoons ground cinnamon**
**5–6 cups milk**

Fill an unbaked pie shell with breadcrumbs. Mix together flour, sugar, and cinnamon, and sprinkle over breadcrumbs. Fill crust with milk to within a ½ inch of the top of the crust. Bake at 375°F about 40 minutes, or until well set.

### LOVINA'S DAUGHTER ELIZABETH

Grandma Coblentz always had Colby cheese with every meal, and my mom does as well. And now I do, too! When we were dating, Tim asked why we always had cheese with a meal, but now he asks for it. My mom and dad would buy horns of cheese from the milkman.

## APRIL 1992,
## ELIZABETH COBLENTZ

The rebirth of the dandelions, nestled in lawns, gardens, pastures, and roadways, are large enough to be eaten now. They always make such a good salad for the evening meal or whenever. Some cooks use dandelions in a gravy, but the best way we like them is with sour cream and hard-cooked eggs. I must say, eating dandelions at an evening meal will really relax someone and help them have a good night's rest.

# Cookies

*This is a moist cookie with a crunch! I omit the raisins because we don't have too many raisin fans in our house.*

## APPLESAUCE COOKIES

**1½ cups lard or shortening**
**2 cups granulated sugar**
**1 egg**
**1 teaspoon baking soda**
**1 teaspoon ground cinnamon**
**½ teaspoon ground cloves**
**⅛ teaspoon salt**
**4–4½ cups all-purpose flour**
**1 cup unsweetened applesauce**
**1 cup raisins**
**1 cup chopped pecans**

In a large bowl, cream together lard and sugar until well combined. Add egg, mixing well. Add baking soda, cinnamon, cloves, salt, and flour and mix well. Add applesauce, raisins, and pecans. Mix until a stiff dough forms, then form into a roll that is about 2½–3 inches thick and wrap in waxed paper; refrigerate for at least 1 hour. Remove waxed paper and cut the roll into slices ½ inch thick. Lay the slices flat on a baking sheet and bake at 375°F for 10–12 minutes.

*These cookies are fun to make and decorate with little ones. They enjoy helping!*

## GINGERBREAD COOKIES

½ cup (1 stick) butter, at room temperature
½ firmly packed cup dark brown sugar
¼ cup dark molasses
1 tablespoon ground cinnamon
2 teaspoons ground cloves
1 teaspoon ground ginger
1 teaspoon baking soda
2 cups all-purpose flour
2 tablespoons water
Baked-on frosting for gingerbread cookies (optional; see below)

In a large bowl, cream together butter, brown sugar, molasses, spices, and baking soda. Blend in the flour and add water as needed, mixing to form a stiff dough. Refrigerate at least 30 minutes.

On a lightly floured surface, roll out dough to ⅛ inch thick (or thinner if you want crisp cookies). Cut dough into desired shapes with cookie cutters dipped in flour. Place 2 inches apart on parchment-lined baking sheets. Bake at 375°F for 8–10 minutes.

If you want to decorate the cookies, frost before baking.

## BAKED-ON FROSTING FOR GINGERBREAD COOKIES

⅔ cup (1 stick plus 3 tablespoons) butter, softened
⅔ cup flour
¼ cup confectioners' sugar
Paste food colors

Beat butter, flour, and confectioners' sugar in a small mixing bowl until smooth. Divide frosting into small bowls and tint each bowl with food color. Transfer frosting to pastry bags and decorate cookies. Bake cookies as directed.

*This cookie dough can be mixed and kept in the refrigerator for up to three days, or in the freezer for three months. Before baking, let the dough sit at room temperature for 30 minutes if dough was frozen, or for 20 minutes if refrigerated.*

## BEST MOLASSES COOKIES

¾ cup (1½ sticks) butter, softened

¾ firmly packed cup brown sugar

¼ cup dark molasses

2 teaspoons vanilla extract

1 egg

2¼ cups flour

1½ teaspoons baking soda

¼ teaspoon salt

2 teaspoons ground ginger

1¼ teaspoons ground cinnamon

¼ teaspoon ground nutmeg

¼ teaspoon ground cloves

⅓ cup granulated sugar, for rolling

In a large bowl, cream together butter and brown sugar. Add molasses, vanilla, and egg and beat until well combined. In another bowl, stir together flour, baking soda, salt, ginger, cinnamon, nutmeg, and cloves. Slowly mix flour mixture into butter mixture until well combined. The dough will be slightly sticky. Cover dough with plastic wrap and refrigerate for at least 1 hour, or up to 3 days.

Remove dough from the refrigerator 20 minutes before you plan to bake the cookies. Preheat oven to 350°F. Take tablespoon-sized portions of dough and roll into balls. Roll balls in sugar and place 3 inches apart on baking sheets. Bake 12 minutes, or until edges appear set and the tops start cracking. Let cookies sit for 5 minutes before removing from baking sheets.

*We make these cookies often to take to church services for the luncheon that is served afterward. My daughter Elizabeth makes these quite often and will bring some to share with us since it makes a nice-sized batch.*

## CHOCOLATE CRINKLES

½ cup confectioners' sugar

2½ cups granulated sugar, divided

1 cup cocoa powder

½ cup butter or oil

4 eggs

2 cups all-purpose flour

2 teaspoons baking powder

½ teaspoon salt

2 teaspoons vanilla extract

Mix together confectioners' sugar and ½ cup granulated sugar and set aside.

In a large bowl, cream together remaining 2 cups granulated sugar, cocoa powder, and butter. Add the eggs, flour, baking powder, salt, and vanilla and mix well. Cover with plastic wrap and refrigerate for at least 2 hours. Roll cookie dough into balls, then roll in prepared sugar mixture and place on baking sheets. Bake at 350°F for 10–12 minutes.

### OCTOBER 1991, ELIZABETH COBLENZ

A lunch is served to all who attend church before they leave for home. Lunch usually consists of coffee, bread, cheese, red beets, pickles, and meat that is usually bologna, wieners, or ham and various spreads such as peanut butter, jelly and jam, butter, apple butter, and sandwich spread. It just depends, as some families serve more and some families serve less. In the summertime there might be sliced tomatoes, radishes, lettuce, and green bell peppers on the lunch menu. At Christmas or Easter you might find some extra baked goodies served.

Two or three tables are set up for each lunch. The young unmarried girls of the church (from age fourteen and up) take care of serving the tables because they need to be reset two or more times. We have a table for the smaller children to help themselves. A milk soup is made for the younger ones.

*If I don't have a fresh lemon on hand, I just use the lemon juice and omit the lemon zest. The lemon juice gives these cookies plenty of good flavor.*

## LEMON CRISPS

1¾ cups (3½ sticks) butter

1 cup granulated sugar

2 eggs

2 teaspoons lemon zest

2 tablespoons lemon juice

5½ cups all-purpose flour

½ teaspoon baking powder

½ teaspoon salt

Cream together butter and sugar, then mix in eggs. Add lemon zest, lemon juice, flour, baking powder, and salt and mix together well. Form into balls. Place on baking sheets and press the balls flat. Bake at 350°F for 10–12 minutes.

**There have been** cooking mix-ups. One time, at the end of a long baking day, my younger girls were putting in the same stuff at the same time. They were going to put in a cup of baking powder in one recipe, and had mixed up baking soda and powder. Daughter Elizabeth had to figure out what they were doing and fix it up. Also, my niece Elizabeth once made frosting with cornstarch instead of confectioners' sugar.

*This cookie is soft and moist, and the pineapple gives it a nice flavor. It's a nice variation from the regular cookies we make.*

## PINEAPPLE COOKIES

**1 cup (2 sticks) butter**
**1 cup granulated sugar**
**1 packed cup brown sugar**
**3 eggs**
**1 (16-ounce can) crushed pineapple, drained**
**1 teaspoon vanilla extract**
**4 cups all-purpose flour**
**1 teaspoon baking soda**
**½ teaspoon salt**
**½ cup chopped pecans (optional)**

Cream together butter, granulated sugar, and brown sugar; add eggs and mix well. Stir in pineapple, vanilla, flour, baking soda, salt, and optional pecans. Drop by teaspoonfuls on lightly greased baking sheets and bake at 375°F for 10 minutes.

Makes about 4 dozen cookies.

*These brownies can be made with or without the frosting. We also like to add chopped nuts on top. The pumpkin is a nice change from regular brownies made from cocoa powder.*

## PUMPKIN BROWNIES

¾ cup (1½ sticks) butter
2 firmly packed cups brown sugar
1 cup pumpkin puree (not pumpkin pie filling)
2 large eggs
2 teaspoons vanilla extract
3⅓ cups flour
1 teaspoon baking powder
1 teaspoon salt
1 teaspoon ground cinnamon
1½ teaspoons pumpkin pie spice
Cream cheese frosting (optional; see below)

In a medium pan, heat butter over medium heat until melted. Add brown sugar and pumpkin and stir until sugar is melted. Set aside to cool.

In a large bowl, beat eggs with a fork; stir in vanilla. Add the cooled pumpkin mixture and stir until combined. Stir in flour, baking powder, salt, cinnamon, and pumpkin pie spice. Pour into a greased 9 x 13-inch pan and bake at 350°F for 35 minutes. Let cool, frost if desired, and cut into bars.

## CREAM CHEESE FROSTING

½ cup (1 stick) butter, softened
1 (8-ounce) package cream cheese
2 cups confectioners' sugar
1 teaspoon vanilla extract

Beat together frosting ingredients until well combined. Spread on cooled brownies.

*I like cookies that can be shaped in a roll and refrigerated until the next day. The next day you can slice the dough, bake, and have fresh-baked cookies! If you don't want to roll the dough, you can place rounded teaspoons of dough directly on baking sheets and bake as directed.*

## REFRIGERATOR COOKIES

**1 cup shortening**
**4 packed cups brown sugar**
**4 eggs**
**2 teaspoons vanilla extract**
**6 cups all-purpose flour**
**1½ teaspoons baking powder**
**1½ teaspoons baking soda**
**1 teaspoon salt**

Cream together shortening and brown sugar, then add eggs and vanilla and mix until fluffy. Mix together flour, baking powder, baking soda, and salt. Add to shortening mixture. If dough is quite sticky, add more flour. Mix until you have smooth, stiff dough. Shape into rolls 2½–3 inches in diameter. Wrap in waxed paper and refrigerate overnight. (There is no need to refrigerate these cookies if you want to bake them right after they are mixed.)

When ready to bake, thinly slice rolls with a sharp knife. Bake on ungreased baking sheets at 400°F for 8 minutes.

Makes about 10 dozen cookies.

*I like to make these cookies around Christmastime, but they are good anytime of year. The nuts give them a nice crunchy texture.*

## SNOWBALL COOKIES

**1 cup (2 sticks) butter, softened**
**½ cup granulated sugar**
**½ teaspoon salt**
**1¼ teaspoons vanilla extract**
**½ cup coarsely chopped walnuts or pecans**
**1¾ cups all-purpose flour**
**Confectioners' sugar, for rolling cookies**

Cream together butter, granulated sugar, salt, and vanilla. Add nuts. Slowly add flour until combined. Wrap dough in plastic wrap and refrigerate several hours.

Preheat oven to 325°F. Drop small scoops of dough onto parchment-lined baking sheets. Bake 10 minutes. Let cool, then roll in confectioners' sugar.

*When my granddaughters eat whoopie pies, they like to pull the cookies apart and eat all the filling and let the cookie parts sit. To make a sour milk substitute, combine 1 tablespoon white vinegar or lemon juice with enough milk to make 1 cup. Let stand 5 minutes.*

## WHOOPIE PIES

**Cookies**
**1 cup hot water**
**2 teaspoons baking soda**
**1 cup butter-flavored shortening**
**2 cups granulated sugar**
**2 eggs**
**1 cup sour milk**
**2 teaspoons vanilla extract**
**4 cups flour**
**½ cup cocoa powder**
**1½ teaspoons salt**

**Filling**
**1 (8-ounce) package cream cheese, softened**
**¼ cup milk**
**2 cups confectioners' sugar**
**1 tablespoon vanilla extract**
**1 (8-ounce) container frozen whipped topping, thawed**

For cookies: Combine hot water and baking soda; set aside and let cool.

In a medium bowl, cream together shortening, sugar, eggs, milk, and vanilla. In another bowl, sift together flour, cocoa powder, and salt. Alternate adding water mixture and flour mixture to shortening mixture, mixing well. Dough may seem too thin, but do not add more flour. Drop tablespoonfuls of batter onto a well-greased baking sheet and bake at 400°F for 8 minutes. Allow to cool.

For filling: Mix cream cheese, milk, confectioners' sugar, and vanilla until smooth. Fold in whipped topping.

Assemble the cookies by spreading a layer of filling on a cooled cookie, then placing another cookie on top.

*These bars are great to take along when you have been invited out and you want to bring a treat. I have covers for a lot of my baking sheets and cake pans, which makes the treats easy to transport in our buggy.*

## RAGGEDY TOP BARS

**1 cup plus 2 tablespoons (2¼ sticks) butter, divided**
**1 firmly packed cup brown sugar**
**1 egg**
**2 teaspoons vanilla extract, divided**
**½ teaspoon salt**
**1¾ cups flour**
**1 cup butterscotch chips**
**⅓ cup light corn syrup**
**¼ teaspoon salt**
**1 cup chopped pecans or walnuts**
**½ cup crushed cornflakes**

In a medium bowl, beat together 1 cup butter and brown sugar. Add egg, 1 teaspoon vanilla, salt, and flour and mix until well blended. Press into a greased 10 x 15-inch pan. Bake at 350°F for 20–25 minutes.

Meanwhile, in a pan over medium heat, melt remaining 2 tablespoons butter, remaining 1 teaspoon vanilla, butterscotch chips, corn syrup, and salt. Stir constantly until butterscotch chips are melted. Stir in nuts and cornflakes. Spread over crust and bake an additional 8 minutes. Cool and cut into bars.

## FEBRUARY 2008

We set up the church benches in our basement for the church services. The benches, dishes for meals, and other supplies needed to hold a service are stored in a wagon that goes from place to place—wherever the services are going to be held. Services are usually around three hours long. Afterward, the menfolk set up four tables, with every table seating sixteen people.

Then the women pitch in and help get the tables set. It is nice to have most of the dishes we need for lunch stored in containers in the bench wagon. Our menu is coffee, tea, homemade wheat and white bread, bologna, cheese spread, peanut butter spread, dill and sweet pickles, red beets, sweet and hot peppers, butter, homemade jam, and sugar, pumpkin, and butterscotch chip cookies.

I also fixed a pot of chicken noodle soup for the younger ones who can't eat sandwiches yet. All in all we had about 150–175 people show up for services, which is a little lower than usual because some people were gone because of sickness.

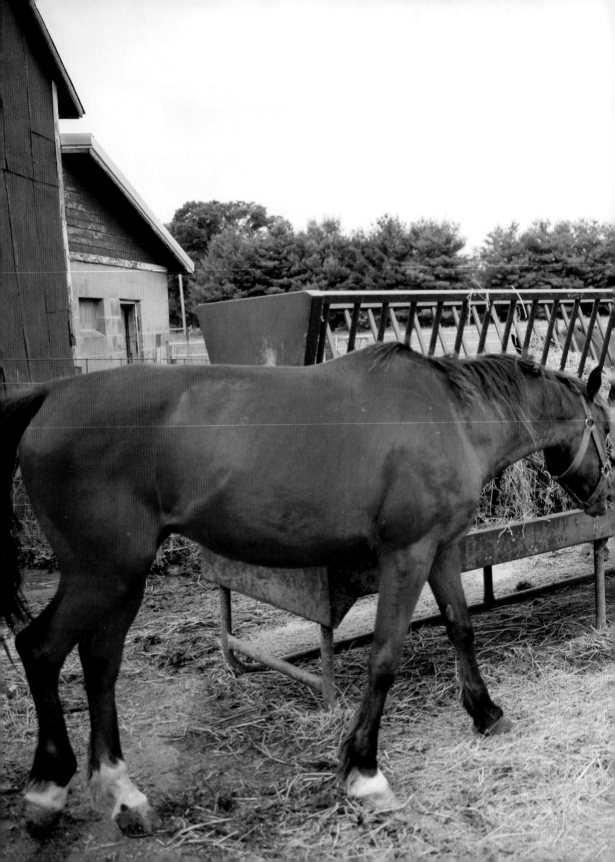

# Desserts

*This is a good combination of blueberries and cherries, but you can choose just one or the other if you prefer. I use my own pints of canned pie filling, but if you buy your filling, it's okay to use the entire can, which is generally more than 1 pint.*

## BLUEBERRY CHERRY SUPREME

¼ pound saltine crackers (1 sleeve from a 1-pound box)
½ cup (1 stick) butter, melted
⅓ cup granulated sugar
1 (8-ounce) package cream cheese, softened
2 cups confectioners' sugar
1 (8-ounce) container frozen whipped topping, thawed
1 pint blueberry pie filling
1 pint cherry pie filling

Preheat oven to 350°F. Crush crackers and combine with melted butter and sugar. Press into a 9 x 13-inch baking pan and bake for 15 minutes. Let cool.

Beat together cream cheese and confectioners' sugar, then fold in thawed whipped topping. Spread on baked cracker mixture. Top with pie fillings, either using one kind on each half or mixing them together. Refrigerate.

### JUNE 2001, ELIZABETH COBLENZ

It's remarkable to watch a barn raising, to see how the barn takes shape, step by step. I've been to several in my lifetime, including our own barn raising while I was still young. I remember there were 126 people—women and children included—who came to help that day. At the time, we thought that 126 was a lot, but compared to nowadays it is not. There are more people around today with all these families, so we might have 250 show up on a day.

A snack of coffee, cookies, and a cold drink is served in the forenoon to all the men, women, and children. At noon, a good lunch is served. Some women bring in all kinds of desserts, casseroles, baked goods, and other food. Long tables are set up in the yard where shade is available, and the food is set on the tables. The food is served cafeteria-style.

In the afternoon another snack, such as cold lemonade and cookies, is passed to everyone. The boys especially enjoy the break. The snack is taken to them after the dishes have been cleared at noon. In the late afternoon, the workers are served a cold drink to quench their thirst on a hot day. Women are usually kept busy caring for the small children.

*We like to drizzle chocolate and butterscotch topping over this dessert. It makes it look yummy and makes it taste great!*

## CREAM PUFF DESSERT

**¾ cup (1½ sticks) butter**
**1½ cups water**
**1½ cups flour**
**6 eggs**
**1 (8-ounce) package cream cheese**
**3 (3.4-ounce) packages vanilla instant pudding**
**4 cups milk**
**1 (16-ounce) container frozen whipped topping, thawed**
**Chocolate syrup, butterscotch topping, grated chocolate, or a combination**

Preheat oven to 400°F.

Put butter and water in a heavy saucepan and place over medium heat. Heat until the butter melts, then bring mixture to a boil. Remove pan from heat and use a wooden spoon to stir in the flour until the mixture pulls away from the sides of the saucepan and forms a soft ball.

Transfer the dough to a large mixing bowl and let it rest for about 5 minutes to cool slightly. Add eggs, one at a time, mixing thoroughly with mixer in between additions. After adding all the eggs, continue to mix 1–2 minutes, or until the dough is smooth.

Transfer the dough to a 10 x 15-inch greased jelly-roll pan. Spread dough out evenly over the bottom of the baking pan. The dough will be sticky. To make it easier to spread, spray the backside of an offset spatula with non-stick cooking spray and use it to spread the dough. Bake for 25–30 minutes, or until the dough puffs up along the sides of the pan and is golden brown. Remove from the oven and cool completely.

Beat the cream cheese, then add instant pudding and milk. Beat until smooth. Spread mixture on cooled crust and cover with whipped topping. Refrigerate at least 1 hour or overnight. Drizzle with chocolate syrup before serving.

*I remember my mom making this pudding on the kerosene cookstove. She would leave it on the cookstove to cool, and we liked to eat it fresh and warm as soon as it cooled down a little.*

## CHOCOLATE PUDDING

**1⅓ cups granulated sugar**
**⅔ cup cocoa powder**
**Pinch salt**
**⅓ cup cornstarch**
**4½ cups whole milk**
**3–4 tablespoons butter**
**1 tablespoon vanilla extract**

In a saucepan, combine sugar, cocoa powder, salt, and cornstarch. Mix well. Add milk and whisk until combined. Cook over medium heat, stirring constantly, until mixture reaches a boil. Let boil for 1 minute, stirring constantly.

Remove from heat and stir in butter and vanilla. Let mixture cool completely, but stir occasionally to avoid a skin forming on the top of the pudding.

*We make this a lot when peaches are in season, but it is good with any fruit. It's always an easy dessert to make.*

---

## EASY FRUIT COBBLER

**½ cup (1 stick) butter, melted and divided**
**1 cup flour**
**1 cup granulated sugar plus additional to sweeten fruit**
**2 teaspoons baking powder**
**¾ cup milk**
**4 cups sliced fruit of your choice**

Coat a 9 x 13-inch baking pan with ¼ cup melted butter. In separate bowl, mix together flour, 1 cup sugar, baking powder, and milk. Add remaining ¼ cup melted butter to flour mixture and stir to mix. Spread into baking pan.

In separate bowl, combine fruit and sugar as desired, depending on sweetness of the fruit. Mix well, then pour over crust in baking dish. Bake at 400°F degrees for 35–40 minutes. May be served hot or cold.

### JULY 2009

Many around here are enjoying homegrown raspberries. They bring back memories of when Mom had her own patch of raspberries that would come up year after year. Mom had red and black raspberries, which she would make into jam. I really liked the jam. She would also make cold soup with them. She would use cold milk, bread, sugar, raspberries, and bananas, which would make a refreshing cold soup on a hot summer day.

*Any fruits can be used on this "pizza." I pick fruits that my family enjoys, especially if they are fresh, in-season fruits.*

## FRUIT PIZZA

**Crust**

¾ cup (1½ sticks) butter

½ cup confectioners' sugar

1½ cups flour

**Filling**

1 (8-ounce) package cream cheese, softened

½ cup granulated sugar

1 teaspoon vanilla extract

**Glaze**

1 cup pineapple juice

1 teaspoon lemon juice

1½ tablespoons cornstarch

**Fruit topping**

Strawberries, blueberries, pineapple, kiwi, grapes, bananas, raspberries

For crust: In a small bowl, beat together butter and sugar until well combined. Add flour and mix well. Pat into a 9 x 13-inch baking dish. Bake at 300°F for 15 minutes. Let cool.

For filling: Mix cream cheese, sugar, and vanilla until well blended. Spread on cooled crust.

For glaze: In a small saucepan, combine pineapple juice, lemon juice, and cornstarch. Stir together and cook over medium heat until mixture comes to a boil and becomes thick.

For fruit topping: Cut up fruit of your choice and arrange on top of cream cheese filling. Drizzle glaze over fruit. Refrigerate until ready to serve.

*This dessert is sometimes served at weddings. The cooks will prepare it a few days in advance and then freeze it until the morning of the wedding. It tastes good on a hot summer day!*

## FRUIT SLUSH

**2 cups granulated sugar**
**3 cups hot water**
**6 ounces frozen orange juice concentrate**
**1 (20-ounce) can crushed pineapple, undrained**
**1 quart canned peaches, chopped and undrained**
**2 (15-ounce) cans mandarin oranges, drained**
**4 bananas, sliced (optional)**

In a large mixing bowl, combine sugar and water until sugar is dissolved. Stir in orange juice concentrate. Add pineapple, peaches, mandarin oranges, and optional bananas. Freeze in single-serving containers or in a large pan or bowl. Thaw slightly before serving.

*Note:* Fresh peaches can be used instead of canned.

*For those of you who like peanut butter pie, this is a good dessert. Homemade pudding is a little more work than store-bought mixes, but the flavor is so much better.*

## PEANUT BUTTER PUDDING

½ cup peanut butter
¾ cup confectioners' sugar
⅔ cup granulated sugar
3 tablespoons cornstarch
1 tablespoon all-purpose flour
Dash salt
3 egg yolks, beaten
3 cups milk
2 tablespoons butter, melted
1 teaspoon vanilla extract

Mix together peanut butter and confectioners' sugar until crumbly. Set aside.

Combine granulated sugar, cornstarch, flour, and salt in a saucepan. In a separate bowl, mix together egg yolks, milk, and butter. Add to sugar mixture in saucepan. Cook over medium heat, stirring often, until thickened. Remove from heat, add vanilla, and cool completely. Layer the pudding and peanut butter mixture in a bowl, repeating layers. Refrigerate and enjoy!

*Note:* Can be layered in a prebaked pie shell and topped with whipped topping.

*I don't always add all the fruits called for in this recipe, but instead use what I have on hand. The mint is optional, but I like the freshness it brings to the fruit.*

## WINTER FRUIT SALAD

**1 cup red grapes**
**1 cup green grapes**
**1 large apple, peeled and sliced**
**1 pear, sliced**
**2 large bananas, peeled and sliced**
**3 kiwis, peeled and sliced**
**3 clementines, peeled and separated**
**½ cup pomegranate seeds (optional)**
**1 tablespoon honey**
**3 tablespoons lime or lemon juice**
**1 tablespoon chopped fresh mint (optional)**

In a large bowl, combine grapes, apple, pear, bananas, kiwis, clementines, and optional pomegranate seeds. Toss lightly. In a small bowl, whisk together honey, lime juice, and optional mint. Drizzle over fruit and toss until coated.

*Note:* You may use any fruit you prefer.

---

### JANUARY 2000, ELIZABETH COBLENZ

I guess there's no reason to complain, if there's plenty of fuel for the stoves. Mixing cut wood with coal makes a good heat. Also, it feels comforting to face the winter with plenty of food to eat. It is good to open the jars which were filled and processed last summer and autumn. We have to do our part. Just like the birds that can't just sit on their nests all the time—they scratch for food too. The good Lord supplies all their needs, and our needs, too! Birds have a great feast on those bird feeders or seeds that are thrown on the ground. Those busy birds live from day to day to be fed. Wouldn't it be hard for us to find our food from day to day? How blessed we are to have a bountiful harvest!

*We love strawberries, so that puts this recipe at the top of my favorite list! This is also a good option for anyone who loves strawberry pie but prefers a graham cracker crust.*

## STRAWBERRY PIE DESSERT

**4 ounces cream cheese**
**½ cup confectioners' sugar**
**2½ cup frozen whipped topping, thawed and divided**
**1 (9-inch) graham cracker crust**
**1 (3-ounce) package strawberry gelatin**
**1 (3-ounce) package cook-and-serve vanilla pudding**
**1¼ cups water**
**2 cups sliced strawberries**

Stir together cream cheese, confectioners' sugar, and ½ cup thawed whipped topping. Spread over graham cracker crust; refrigerate.

In a saucepan, mix together gelatin, vanilla pudding, and water. Bring to a boil, stirring often, and continue cooking until smooth. Remove from heat and let cool 5 minutes. Stir in strawberries and pour over cream cheese mixture in crust. Refrigerate for 4 hours. Top with 2 cups additional whipped topping.

## JUNE 2008

For my birthday gift Joe got me a fishing license, fishing pole, and a life jacket. This is the first fishing license I have ever had. I have never taken an interest in fishing, but Joe wants to take me out on the lake fishing to see if he can get me interested. I have never been out on a boat before, and I can't swim, so he wanted me to have a life jacket.

Fish makes a very economical, tasty supper. Our children like fish best when I put it in batter and deep-fry it. With meat prices being so high, the more fish we get helps cut down on the grocery bill.

Miscellaneous

*Canned tomato can be used for this recipe, but fresh tomato is best. This is similar to a traditional guacamole but with the addition of the fun flavors of green bell pepper and paprika.*

## AVOCADO SALSA

**1 ripe avocado**
**1 green bell pepper**
**1 small onion**
**1 large tomato**
**1 teaspoon salt**
**¼ teaspoon garlic powder**
**¼ teaspoon paprika**
**Hot peppers, chopped (optional)**

Chop avocado, bell pepper, onion, and tomato. Mix together and add salt, garlic powder, paprika, and optional hot peppers. Adjust seasoning to taste.

*I serve this in a glass pie pan for easy dipping. The toppings of cheese, tomatoes, and onions look good on top. I like using both the white and the green parts of the green onion. If you like garlic, you can try adding another clove.*

## GARLIC DIP

**2 (8-ounce) packages cream cheese, softened**

**½ cup sour cream**

**¼ cup mayonnaise**

**1 clove garlic, minced**

**1 bunch cilantro, chopped**

**1½ cups shredded cheddar cheese, divided**

**½ cup chopped tomatoes**

**2 tablespoons chopped green onions**

Mix together cream cheese, sour cream, mayonnaise, garlic, cilantro, and 1 cup cheddar cheese. Put in a serving dish. Top with remaining ½ cup cheddar cheese, tomatoes, and green onions. Serve with crackers or vegetables.

**Microwave popcorn** is a real treat. We would have a bowl of popcorn with cheddar seasoning or sour cream and onion seasoning. When Tim and Liz started going together, he would season it with whatever seasoning we had. Soon it was "Tim's popcorn," and the other was just "popcorn." We also usually have popcorn on Sunday afternoons. Someone brings sandwich bags of popcorn every time we have church.

*We like salsa on breakfast burritos, tacos, haystacks, and chips, so we make a lot of salsa each year when the vegetables are ripe in our garden.*

## FRESH SALSA

**5 roma tomatoes**
**3 hot peppers**
**1 small onion**
**1 clove garlic, minced**
**1 tablespoon minced cilantro**
**¼ teaspoon salt**
**¼ teaspoon black pepper**
**½ teaspoon lemon juice**

Finely chop the tomatoes, hot peppers, and onion. Add remaining ingredients and mix well; refrigerate overnight. Serve with chips.

*We like this on our grilled or baked meats, especially chicken and pork. This recipe is often used at weddings, although in much larger amounts.*

## HOMEMADE BARBECUE SAUCE

**1½ cups ketchup**
**½ cup honey**
**¼ cup white vinegar**
**½ tablespoon prepared mustard**
**1 tablespoon minced garlic**
**½ tablespoon minced onion**
**¼ cup salt**

Heat all ingredients together in a saucepan on the stove, and stir until blended. Let cool and refrigerate until ready to use.

### JULY 1992, ELIZABETH COBLENZ

I turned a year older on July 18. My daughter Emma turned a year older on July 19. Our family enjoyed a barbecued chicken and steak supper on my birthday. Of course, ice cream and cake had to be on the menu also. My son Amos brought it and our daughter Leah brought a skillet and whoopie pies. Susan made zucchini squash bread.

*Marinating meat always seems to make the meat juicier and more tender. Marinate for at least thirty minutes if you can, but if you don't have several hours to marinate you can still use this recipe—just marinate for a shorter amount of time. The flavor won't be as intense, but it will still be good! The marinade is good for preparing chicken or steaks for the grill. It makes a large batch, but it can be stored in the refrigerator.*

## MEAT MARINADE

⅓ scant cup salt

2 cups white vinegar

2 cups water

1 cup oil

2 tablespoons Worcestershire sauce

2 tablespoons soy sauce

1 tablespoon lemon juice

1 teaspoon red hot sauce

Mix all ingredients thoroughly. Add meat and marinate for several hours.

**My grandparents** didn't eat much for dinner, usually just sandwiches. Sometimes they'd dip their sandwiches in water, and sometimes my grandma would dip hers in coffee soup.

*I like to have a few recipes on hand that use fruit and honey instead of lots of sugar, and this is a good one. If you don't have fresh strawberries you can use frozen ones, but drain them before adding so that the dip doesn't get too soupy. You can use low-fat cream cheese instead of regular.*

## STRAWBERRY DIP

**1 (8-ounce) package cream cheese, softened**
**2 tablespoons honey**
**1 teaspoon vanilla extract**
**1 pint strawberries, sliced**

In a bowl, beat together cream cheese, honey, and vanilla until smooth. Add strawberries; beat 1 minute. Serve with graham crackers.

Makes about 2 cups.

### JUNE 1996, ELIZABETH COBLENZ

Some time ago, friends of ours from Costa Rica were in the area and gave us coffee from Costa Rica. So I made some to serve for the big noon lunch after church. Also, I made some spearmint tea for lunch, which grows well here. We also served ham, cheese, lettuce, red beets, pickles, margarine, apple butter, sandwich spread, rhubarb jam, peanut butter mixture, and home-baked white and wheat bread (the wheat bread was made by my sister Lovina). It was all delicious!

*I remember my mother making eggnog a lot during the winter months. I don't remember her cooking the egg mixture, but it seems now it is recommended it be cooked rather than using raw eggs in the recipe.*

## SAFE HOMEMADE EGGNOG

**6 eggs**
**¼ cup granulated sugar**
**4 cups skim milk, divided**
**1 teaspoon vanilla extract**
**Garnishes and stir-ins (see instructions)**

In a large saucepan, beat together eggs and sugar. Stir in 2 cups milk. Cook over low heat, stirring constantly, until mixture is thick enough to coat a metal spoon with a thin layer or the mixture reaches at least 160°F on a cooking thermometer. Remove from heat. Stir in remaining 2 cups milk along with the vanilla. Cover and refrigerate until thoroughly chilled—several hours or overnight. Just before serving, pour into a bowl or pitcher.

If desired, garnish each cup or stir in grated nutmeg, chocolate curls, cinnamon sticks, orange slices, candy canes, sherbet, ice cream, or whipped cream.

Makes about 1½ quarts.

*We usually make this around the Christmas holiday. I like to put some in little glass containers and give as gifts to family and friends. A small ribbon wrapped around the neck of the jar makes it especially festive.*

## TOASTED PECAN CLUSTERS

**2 tablespoons butter**

**2–3 cups coarsely chopped pecans**

**1 pound chocolate candy coating (milk chocolate, semi-sweet, or a combination)**

Put butter on a 10 x 15-inch jelly-roll pan and place in 300°F oven until butter is melted. When butter is melted, toss with chopped pecans. Toast in the oven at 300°F for 10–15 minutes, stirring several times, until nuts are lightly toasted. Remove from oven and allow to cool.

Melt candy coating in a double boiler, stirring until completely melted. Stir in cooled, toasted pecans. Drop by teaspoonfuls onto waxed paper. Refrigerate until set, and store in the refrigerator.

**I remember** getting together at my grandmother's house for New Year's celebrations. We gathered together outside and sang the New Year's song, then they would have a huge full-course meal. She made Limburger cheese, but we didn't like it. She kept it in a special glass container.

Family
Picnics

*We plant sweet banana peppers to use for these, but a few of us like the hot banana peppers. A little minced garlic or garlic powder in the cream cheese is a nice addition. You will need strong round toothpicks to hold these poppers together.*

## BANANA PEPPER POPPERS

**Banana peppers, however many you want to prepare**
**1–2 (8-ounce) packages cream cheese, softened**
**2–4 cups shredded cheddar cheese (8–16 ounces)**
**Thick-sliced bacon, 1 slice per pepper**

Remove seeds from peppers (if peppers are spicy, wear rubber gloves to prevent hands from burning). Mix cream cheese and shredded cheese and stuff into peppers. Wrap each pepper with 1 slice bacon, using toothpicks to hold it in place. Grill until bacon is done, turning a few times.

**There are six girls** in my family, so we became good at making certain things. I always made the bread, one of my sisters made the pies, one loved to make cookies and rolls. My own five daughters have specialties too. Susan always made baked French toast, and Loretta loves to grill. She loves to grill whole chickens with mushrooms and little red potatoes, and she loves to grill banana pepper poppers. Loretta loves to dip each one in hot sauce.

*This is a good campfire meal, but we make kabobs on the grill too. The Italian dressing coats them so they don't burn as quickly. We also soak the wooden skewers in water for about ten minutes so they won't burn.*

## CAMPFIRE SHISH KABOBS

**Shrimp**

**Bacon**

**Mushrooms**

**Sweet peppers**

**Onions**

**Pineapple**

**Italian dressing**

**Salt and pepper**

Cut meat, vegetables, and fruit into 1-inch chunks (shrimp can remain whole) and marinate in Italian dressing for a couple of hours. Place items on skewers in rotating order. Sprinkle with salt and pepper as desired. Roast over a fire until meat is cooked through.

*I like meals where there are no pots or pans to clean up afterward. After you assemble these you can sit and relax around the campfire, or you can grill while these are cooking. You will need eight sheets of heavy duty aluminum foil cut into 18-inch pieces. Make sure to seal the foil tightly so the liquid doesn't leak out.*

## CAMPFIRE CHICKEN MEALS

**1 pound thick bacon, cut into 1-inch pieces**

**3 large potatoes, cut into 1-inch pieces**

**5 carrots, peeled and cut into ½-inch pieces**

**1 (15-ounce) can sweet peas, drained**

**1 (15¼-ounce) can whole kernel corn, drained**

**4 boneless, skinless chicken breasts, cut into 1-inch pieces**

**1 cup chicken broth, or 1 cube chicken bouillon dissolved in 1 cup water**

**1 teaspoon garlic salt**

**1 teaspoon onion powder**

**Salt and pepper**

Brown bacon, drain, and set aside.

In the following order, place on four 18-inch pieces of heavy duty aluminum foil: potatoes, carrots, peas, corn. Divide chicken evenly and place on top of vegetables. Top with bacon.

Combine broth, garlic salt, and onion powder, and season with salt and pepper as desired. Pour ¼ cup broth onto each foil. (It may help to fold up the sides of the foil.) Place a second sheet of foil on top of the food and fold to make four pouches. Seal tightly. Place in campfire and cook for 30 minutes. Remove from fire and open carefully.

Serves 4.

*I usually have all these ingredients in the house so that it's easy to double or triple this recipe depending on who will be here for dinner. We often have our married children stay for dinner at the last minute, so it comes in handy to have a solar-powered freezer filled with plenty of meats and vegetables, and shelves filled with home-canned goods in the basement.*

## GRILLED OR BAKED POTATO STICKS

**4 potatoes**
**1 tablespoon oil**
**½ teaspoon paprika**
**⅛ teaspoon garlic powder**
**⅛ teaspoon onion powder**
**Salt and pepper**

Leave skins on the potatoes and slice them lengthwise into eighths. Line a shallow baking pan with aluminum foil. Combine oil and spices in pan, seasoning with salt and pepper as desired, and toss well to coat potatoes. Bake at 325°F or grill for 1 hour.

Serves 4.

### OCTOBER 1995, ELIZABETH COBLENZ

Sunday evenings aren't usually dull around here. Sometimes we never know who will show up for the evening meal. We are glad to see our married children come home! This past Sunday we had pork steak, ham, and sausage on the grill, with mashed potatoes, gravy, and frozen corn. We prepared the meal with this and that from the garden. There were thirty-three family members here to feast on Sunday night, and it was an enjoyable evening.

*Loretta's special friend, Dustin, made this for us one night. We named it Dustin's Skillet because he didn't have a name for it and just added what he thought would taste good. We now make it often because it has become a family favorite.*

## DUSTIN'S SKILLET

**1 pound breakfast sausage**
**1 pound bacon, cut into small pieces**
**12 ounces shrimp, cooked with tails cut off**
**2 green bell peppers, chopped**
**1 medium onion, chopped**
**8 ounces fresh mushrooms, sliced**

In a skillet, fry sausage, bacon, and shrimp until sausage and bacon are cooked through. Drain drippings; return skillet to burner. Add chopped peppers and onions. Cook briefly. Add sliced mushrooms and stir until vegetables are hot.

**My sister Emma**, the second youngest, remembers this: When I first got married I made liver and onions. My husband said, "This doesn't taste like your mom's." I had to go home and ask my mom how to make liver and onions. It turns out that I hadn't made the grease hot enough, and I left the liver in too long so it got rubbery.

*This is a favorite for us when we make supper on the grill. On hot summer nights when it's too hot to cook inside, this works great for a meal! You can make individual aluminum foil packs or wrap food tightly in one large foil pack.*

## SUPPER ON THE GRILL

**1 pound steak, cut into 1-inch cubes**

**1 pound bacon, cut into small pieces**

**12 ounces shrimp, tails removed (optional)**

**1 medium onion, chopped**

**1 green bell pepper, chopped**

**8 ounces mushrooms, cut up**

**6 medium potatoes, cubed**

**1 cup olive oil**

**Salt and pepper**

Mix everything together, seasoning with salt and pepper and any additional seasonings as desired. Toss until seasoning is well mixed with the meat and vegetables. Wrap in aluminum foil and grill until meat is cooked through and potatoes are soft.

Makes about 12 servings.

# Family Reunion Meals

EICHER FA

VERENA
DUSTIN & LORETTA
Benjamin          JOSEPH
              Joseph
          Lovina
Abigail
Kevin
                  Jae & Lovina
        Lovina                  LOVINA

              Lovina

                              Kevin
                              Lovina
JOSEPH

              JOSEPH
              KEVIN
Kevin
        Verena
VERENA          JOSEPH
                    KEVIN
              Lovina
        KEVIN

        Kevin  KEVIN
Lovina          Jae & Lovina
        TIMOTHY & ELIZABETH


ILY  *2017*

*I don't think you can have a family reunion without baked beans. If you'd like, you can add some fried bacon for extra flavor.*

## BAKED BEANS

**4 gallons pork 'n' beans**
**2 cups diced onion**
**4½ packed cups brown sugar**
**3 cups granulated sugar**
**1½ cups ketchup**

Mix ingredients together and heat in an electric roaster at 250°F. Bring to a boil, then let simmer for 3–4 hours.

Serves 100.

**Sometimes we make** coffee soup, which is instant coffee, milk, and sugar. Some of us add cracker crumbs or break up toast and put it in. My husband, Joe, pours his coffee soup over his eggs and potatoes.

*This is a really big recipe, but you can adjust the ingredients to make a smaller batch. We love chocolate chip cookies, and the children often ask if they can try one when they are still warm from the oven.*

## CHOCOLATE CHIP COOKIES

**4 cups butter or margarine**

**4 packed cups brown sugar**

**4 cups granulated sugar**

**8 eggs**

**8 teaspoons vanilla extract**

**12 cups all-purpose flour**

**4 teaspoons baking soda**

**4 teaspoons salt**

**10 cups chocolate chips**

**4 cups chopped walnuts or pecans**

In a large mixing bowl, cream together butter and brown and granulated sugars. Add eggs one at a time, mixing after each one. Mix in vanilla. Combine flour, baking soda, and salt, then mix into the butter mixture a few cups at a time until well combined. Stir in chocolate chips and nuts. Drop by teaspoonfuls onto a greased baking sheet. Bake at 400°F for 10–12 minutes, or until lightly browned.

*This is a nice big cake for reunions or if you have a big group of people you need to make a dessert for. If you need a substitution for buttermilk, put 1 tablespoon white vinegar or lemon juice in a 1-cup liquid measuring cup, then add enough milk to bring the liquid to the 1-cup line. Let stand 5 minutes.*

## CHOCOLATE CAKE

3 cups all-purpose flour
2 cups granulated sugar
1 cup cocoa powder
2 teaspoons baking soda
2 teaspoons baking powder
1 cup sour cream or buttermilk
1 cup shortening
2 eggs, beaten
1 teaspoon vanilla extract
1 cup boiling water

Mix together flour, sugar, cocoa powder, baking soda, and baking powder. In another large bowl, cream together sour cream and shortening. Mix in eggs and vanilla.

Mix flour mixture into sour cream mixture, then stir in boiling water. Pour into a greased 10 x 15-inch jelly-roll pan and bake at 350°F for 30–40 minutes.

### JULY 1995, ELIZABETH COBLENZ

Well, my fifty-ninth birthday is history. Our family got together last night for my birthday. I planned a haystack meal, which consisted of cheese sauce, cooked spaghetti, diced green bell peppers, carrots, onions, tomatoes, celery, crushed cracker crumbs, and browned hamburger layered in a dish. We also had fresh peas, green beans, grilled beef steak, ice cream, cake, cucumber salad, buttered red beets, one-kettle soup, Jell-O, and fruit salad. The folding table was full and there was plenty to eat. We had food in the shed, and folding tables were also set up in the yard for people to eat at. What a nice and relaxing evening to be all together.

*I remember my mother often making these rolls when I was growing up. I loved to watch her spread the butter on the dough, then sprinkle the brown sugar and cinnamon on it. After I was married I asked Mother if she could give me the recipe. She sat down and wrote it on one of my recipe cards. She knew the recipe without even looking. I once made them when I was in a hurry, and I forgot to add the cinnamon, so I just sprinkled it on top of the rolls while they were rising. I made a frosting for the rolls so my mistake was hidden, and no one could tell the difference. They turned out great!*

## MOTHER'S SWEET ROLLS

1½ cups milk, scalded

½ cup (1 stick) butter

½ cup granulated sugar

2 teaspoons salt

4½ teaspoons (2 packages) active
   dry yeast

½ cup warm water

3 eggs, beaten

6 cups bread flour

Butter, softened

Brown sugar

Cinnamon

In a large bowl, combine scalded milk, ½ cup butter, sugar, and salt.

Add yeast to the warm water and let stand 5 minutes, then add it to milk mixture. Making sure the milk isn't too hot, add eggs, then stir in 3 cups flour. Add remaining 3 cups flour and mix well.

Let dough rise until doubled in size. Punch down and divide dough in two. Roll each part out and spread with softened butter. Sprinkle with brown sugar and cinnamon as desired. Roll up lengthwise and cut into ¾-inch slices. Place each piece on a baking pan and let rise until doubled in size. Bake at 350°F for 15 minutes, or until golden brown.

**My mother** would make cinnamon rolls once or twice a month, and we'd have them for breakfast or as a dessert. She'd also serve them to the groups of people (non-Amish visitors) she'd have to her house for a meal. There would be homemade pies and breads, sweet rolls, chicken and dressing, and all kinds of salads. My sisters and I would get on the tour bus and yodel for the visitors.

*I like to let the flavors come together, so I prefer to make my potato salad the day before we will eat it so that it is nice and chilled. If the potato salad is going to be served at an outdoor picnic, I fill a disposable pan with ice and set the bowl on top of the ice to keep it from spoiling.*

## ONE-GALLON POTATO SALAD

**5 pounds potatoes, peeled, boiled, and shredded**
**12 hard-cooked eggs, chopped**
**2 cups chopped celery**
**1 large onion, chopped**
**3 cups salad dressing**
**3 teaspoons prepared mustard**
**¼ cup vinegar**
**½ cup milk**
**1½ cups granulated sugar**
**4 teaspoons salt**

Mix together the potatoes, eggs, celery, and onion. In another bowl, mix together the salad dressing, mustard, vinegar, milk, sugar, and salt. Pour over potato mixture and stir until well combined.

*This makes a very large batch, so it is perfect for a large family gathering. We have family reunions often, and because Joe and I are both from large families, I am always looking for recipes that serve a lot of people.*

## SCALLOPED POTATOES AND HAM

**20 pounds potatoes, cooked and shredded**

**10 pounds ham, cubed**

**4 (10½-ounce) cans cream of mushroom soup**

**4 (10-ounce) cans cheddar cheese soup**

**2 (10½-ounce) cans cream of celery soup**

**2 (12-ounce) cans evaporated milk**

**1½ cups milk**

**2 teaspoons salt**

**1 teaspoon black pepper**

Combine potatoes and ham. Mix together soups, evaporated milk, milk, salt, and pepper, then add to potatoes and ham. Mix together, but avoid over-stirring. Put into a 4-inch chafer pan or an electric roaster. Bake at 325°F for 1½ hours (2½ hours if dish has been refrigerated beforehand). Allow 2 hours for electric roaster (3 hours if refrigerated), adjusting temperature as necessary.

Makes 75 servings.

# Cooking with Children

*We love plain pretzels as a snack, but the children especially like the flavor of them when I make this recipe.*

## CHEESY PRETZELS

**2 pounds pretzels**
**1 cup vegetable oil**
**¾ cup sour cream**
**¾ cup onion powder**
**½ cup granulated sugar**
**½ cup cheddar cheese powder**

Place the pretzels in a large roasting pan. In a separate bowl, stir together remaining ingredients and pour over pretzels. Mix well. Bake in a 200°F oven for 1 hour, stirring every 15 minutes.

### MARCH 2009

While we were in sister Emma and Jacob's garage cutting up their meat, their two boys and our Benjamin and Joseph were in the barnyard having a grand time. Jacob went out to check on them and discovered that they had a long rope tied to their untrained pony's halter. To the other end of the rope they had tied their sled. All four boys were on the sled, and the pony was galloping around the field. They were enjoying the fast sled ride, but did not think about the danger that could happen with the long rope. Jacob soon stopped them, and we were all thankful that no one was hurt. What imaginations children have sometimes!

*We take these along if we are going on a picnic and put them on the grill until they are heated through. They are so easy to cook because they can be made ahead of time.*

## FILLED WIENER BUNS

**8 hot dogs, diced**
**1 cup shredded or diced cheese**
**½ small onion, diced**
**1 tablespoon ketchup**
**1 tablespoon prepared mustard**
**1 teaspoon pickle relish**
**8 hot dog buns**

Mix first six ingredients and fill the hot dog buns. Wrap in foil and bake at 325°F for 15 minutes.

This recipe can be made in advance and frozen, but allow for a longer baking time.

*I made these a lot when the children were younger. They loved helping me make the hole in the bread! I am glad I let the children help me when they were younger, even though I probably could have made the recipes quicker without their help. It was time we got to spend together, and it taught them to enjoy cooking and baking at an early age.*

## EGG IN THE NEST

**1 slice bread**
**1 tablespoon butter, softened**
**1 egg**
**Salt and pepper**

Butter both sides of the bread, then use a biscuit cutter or the rim of a glass to press a hole in the center of the slice. Remove the circle.

Warm skillet over medium heat, then place the bread in the pan. Crack the egg into the hole in the bread. Cook until the white is set, then flip over and cook for another 1–2 minutes.

You can toast the cut-out circle of bread in the pan next to the bread and egg. Turn the circle when you flip the bread, and serve them together so that the circle can be dipped into the egg yolk.

### LOVINA'S DAUGHTER ELIZABETH

When we were children, we would go out to one of the cows carrying a cup. Dad would squirt milk right from the cow into our cup, and we would drink it warm from the cow.

*This is a treat our girls like to make when our little granddaughters are here. They love sprinkling the marshmallows, chocolate chips, and M&M's onto the dough—although they enjoy sampling the most!*

## PIZZA BAR COOKIES

¼ cup (½ stick) butter, softened

½ cup granulated sugar

⅓ packed cup brown sugar

1 egg

1 teaspoon vanilla extract

½ cup peanut butter

1½ cups all-purpose flour

1 (10½-ounce) bag colored miniature marshmallows

1½ cups chocolate chips

⅔ cup mini M&M's

Cream together the butter and granulated and brown sugars. Add egg and vanilla; mix well. Stir in peanut butter, then add flour, mixing well. Press or roll dough into a 9 x 13-inch baking pan and bake at 375°F for 10 minutes. Remove from oven. Add marshmallows, chocolate chips, and M&M's. Return to oven for 5–8 minutes. Cut into bars when cool.

**I was going** to town to get groceries one day, so I asked daughter Elizabeth if she'd make a double batch of peanut butter cookies. I wrote the recipe out on a card for her and doubled the recipe so it would be easier for her to do. Elizabeth, however, didn't realize I had already doubled the recipe for her. So she doubled my "double recipe." So I had more than enough cookies to take to Emma's, plus enough for our own family!

*Finger Jigglers are an easy snack and always a favorite with the little ones. We like to make a variety of flavors. I use Knox gelatin*

## FINGER JIGGLERS

**4 (1-ounce) envelopes unflavored gelatin**
**3 (3¼-ounce) packages flavored gelatin of your choice**
**4 cups boiling water**

Combine the gelatins in a bowl. Pour in the boiling water and stir until gelatin is dissolved. Pour into a 9 x 13-inch pan, cover with plastic wrap, and refrigerate until set, about 2 hours. Cut into squares and serve.

*When we have fresh green onions from the garden this is a good way to use them up. We like Miracle Whip or ranch dressing better than mayonnaise.*

## TORTILLA ROLL-UPS

2 (8-ounce) packages cream cheese, softened
⅓ cup mayonnaise
2–3 tablespoons thinly sliced green onions
10 large tortillas
1 cup shredded cheese
40 slices cooked ham

Combine cream cheese, mayonnaise, and green onions; mix well. Spread a thin layer of the cream cheese mixture on each tortilla. Sprinkle with shredded cheese. Arrange 4 ham slices over each tortilla. Roll up tightly and wrap each roll in plastic wrap. Refrigerate 3 hours or longer. To serve, cut each roll into ¾-inch diagonal slices.

### LOVINA'S SISTER SUSAN COBLENTZ, ELIZABETH'S YOUNGEST DAUGHTER

Mom was a very good cook, and I still miss her cooking. After she passed, nothing tasted as good as her cooking. When I was in sixth grade I had to make a recipe. She helped me make potato salad, mixing it all together.

**My children** remember my mom sitting on the back steps cracking English walnuts. They would play doctor with her, wrapping her feet in bandages while she cracked nuts.

# INDEX

**A**

Apples
  Sour Cream Apple Pie, 142
Applesauce Cookies, 148
Asparagus
  Creamed Ham and Asparagus, 114
Autumn Vegetable Dish, 106
Avocado Salsa, 186

**B**

Bacon
  Bacon and Egg Bake, 24
  Bacon Bean Soup, 64
  Bacon Fried Cabbage, 108
  Banana Pepper Poppers, 200
  Breakfast Omelet Roll, 32
  Cheesy Baked Eggs, 31
  Chicken Meals, Campfire, 204
  Dustin's Skillet, 206
  Egg Omelet, 26
  Lettuce Salad, Layered, 117
  Shish Kabobs, Campfire, 203
  Spaghetti Casserole, Baked, 85
  Supper on the Grill, 209
  Turkey Hash, 99
Baked Barbecue Ribs, 82
Baked Beans, 212
Banana Cake Bars, Frosted, 133
Banana Cornbread Pancakes, 38
Banana Pepper Poppers, 200
Barbecue Ribs, Baked, 82
Barbecue Sauce, Homemade, 190

Bars
  Banana Cake Bars, Frosted, 133
  Pizza Bar Cookies, 229
  Raggedy Top Bars, 162
  Vegetable Bars, 110
Beans
  Bacon Bean Soup, 64
  Baked Beans, 212
  Vegetable Soup, 69
  Zucchini Bean Salad, 121
Beef
  Cabbage Rolls, 86
  Goulash, Good, 87
  Green Bean Casserole, 92
  Hamburger Gravy, 113
  Hearty Hamburger Soup, 68
  Pizza Burgers, 75
  Spaghetti Casserole, Baked, 85
  Supper on the Grill, 209
  Swiss Steak, 98
  Vegetable Soup, 69
  Zucchini Pizza Casserole, 100
Berries
  Blueberry Cherry Supreme, 168
  Strawberry Dip, 192
  Strawberry Pie Dessert, 180
Beverages
  Eggnog, Safe Homemade, 194
Blueberry Cherry Supreme, 168
Breads and bread dishes
  Banana Cornbread Pancakes, 38
  Bread Pie, Poor Man's, 143

Caramel Dumplings, 46
Crust for Fruit Pizza, 174
Doughnuts, 44
Egg in the Nest, 226
French Toast, Crunchy Crust, 36
Garlic Bubble Loaf, 47
Monkey Bread, 48
Muffins, Morning Maple, 50
Peach Bread, 52
Pizza Dough, My Favorite, 49
Pumpkin Cinnamon Rolls, 55
Sweet Rolls, Mother's, 216
White Bread, 58
Wiener Buns, Filled, 225
Zucchini Bread, 57
Breakfast and brunch
Bacon and Egg Bake, 24
Banana Cornbread Pancakes, 38
Breakfast Brunch, 28
Breakfast Casserole with White Sauce, 29
Breakfast Omelet in a Skillet, 30
Breakfast Omelet Roll, 32
Cheesy Baked Eggs, 31
Cinnamon Pecan Coffee Cake,
   Overnight, 39
Crunchy Crust French Toast, 36
Egg in the Nest, 226
Egg Omelet, 26
Goldenrod Eggs, 25
Scrambled Egg Muffins, 35
Broth
Campfire Chicken Meals, 204
Chicken Potpie, 91
Potato Onion Cheese Soup, 73
Turkey Hash, 99
Brown Butter Gravy, 109
Brownies, Pumpkin, 156
Butterscotch
Raggedy Top Bars, 162

## C

Cabbage
  Bacon Fried Cabbage, 108
  Cabbage Rolls, 86
  Coleslaw Pasta Salad, 122
  Ham and Cabbage Soup, 66
Cakes
  Chocolate Cake, 214
  Cinnamon Pecan Coffee Cake,
    Overnight, 39
  Frosted Banana Cake Bars, 133
  Maple Sugar Cake, 129
  Pear Cake, 131
  Sugar Crumb Cake, 132
Campfire Chicken Meals, 204
Caramel Cinnamon Roll Frosting, 56
Caramel Dumplings, 46
Carrots
  Carrots and Onions, 112
  Chicken Meals, Campfire, 204
Casseroles
  Breakfast, with White Sauce, 29
  Chicken, Overnight, 93
  Green Bean, 92
  Spaghetti, Baked, 85
  Zucchini Pizza, 100
Cereal
  Crunchy Crust French Toast, 36
  Raggedy Top Bars, 162
Cheese. *See also* Cream cheese
  Banana Pepper Poppers, 200
  Breakfast Brunch, 28
  Breakfast Casserole with White Sauce, 29
  Cheese Soup, Mom's, 70
  Cheesy Baked Eggs, 31
  Cheesy Pretzels, 224
  Garlic Dip, 187
  Ham and Cheese Sticky Buns, 76
  Pizza Burgers, 75

Potato Onion Cheese Soup, 73
  Ranch Potatoes, 116
  Zucchini Pizza Casserole, 100
Cherries
  Blueberry Cherry Supreme, 168
  Cherry Pie, 135
Chicken
  Casserole, Overnight, 93
  Hot Wings, 88
  Meals, Campfire, 204
  Potpie, 91
  Sweet and Spicy Baked, 96
Chicken broth
  Campfire Chicken Meals, 204
  Chicken Potpie, 91
  Potato Onion Cheese Soup, 73
Children, cooking with
  Cheesy Pretzels, 224
  Egg in the Nest, 226
  Filled Wiener Buns, 225
  Finger Jigglers, 230
  Pizza Bar Cookies, 229
  Tortilla Roll-Ups, 231
Chocolate
  Cake, 214
  Chocolate Chip Cookies, 213
  Chocolate Crinkles, 153
  Pecan Clusters, Toasted, 195
  Pudding, 172
  Whoopie Pies, 161
Cilantro
  Garlic Dip, 187
Cinnamon
  Cinnamon Pecan Coffee Cake,
    Overnight, 39
  Monkey Bread, 48
  Pumpkin Cinnamon Rolls, 55
Coconut
  Oatmeal Pie, 139
Coleslaw Pasta Salad, 122

Cookies
Applesauce, 148
Chocolate Chip, 213
Chocolate Crinkles, 153
Gingerbread, 149
Lemon Crisps, 154
Molasses, Best, 150
Pineapple, 155
Pizza Bar, 229
Pumpkin Brownies, 156
Raggedy Top Bars, 162
Refrigerator, 157
Snowball, 158
Whoopie Pies, 161
Cornflakes
Crunchy Crust French Toast, 36
Raggedy Top Bars, 162
Cream cheese
Banana Pepper Poppers, 200
Blueberry Cherry Supreme, 168
Cream Puff Dessert, 171
Frosting, 156
Fruit Pizza, 174
Garlic Dip, 187
Strawberry Dip, 192
Strawberry Pie Dessert, 180
Tortilla Roll-Ups, 231
Cream of celery soup
Scalloped Potatoes and Ham, 218
Cream of mushroom soup
Bacon and Egg Bake, 24
Overnight Chicken Casserole, 93
Scalloped Potatoes and Ham, 218
Cream Puff Dessert, 171
Crunchy Crust French Toast, 36

**D**
Desserts. *See also* Cakes; Cookies; Pies, sweet
Blueberry Cherry Supreme, 168
Chocolate Pudding, 172
Cream Puff Dessert, 171
Fruit Cobbler, Easy, 173
Fruit Pizza, 174
Fruit Salad, Winter, 178
Fruit Slush, 176
Peanut Butter Pudding, 177
Strawberry Pie Dessert, 180
Dips and sauces
Avocado Salsa, 186
Barbecue Sauce, Homemade, 190
Garlic Dip, 187
for Goldenrod Eggs, 25
Meat Marinade, 191
Salsa, Fresh, 188
Strawberry Dip, 192
White Sauce for Breakfast Casserole, 29
Doughnuts, 44
Dressing for Coleslaw Pasta Salad, 122
Dumplings, Caramel, 46
Dustin's Skillet, 206

**E**

Egg dishes
  Bacon and Egg Bake, 24
  Breakfast Brunch, 28
  Breakfast Casserole with White Sauce, 29
  Breakfast Omelet in a Skillet, 30
  Breakfast Omelet Roll, 32
  Cheesy Baked Eggs, 31
  Cream Puff Dessert, 171
  Egg in the Nest, 226
  Eggnog, Safe Homemade, 194
  Egg Omelet, 26
  Goldenrod Eggs, 25
  Lettuce Salad, Layered, 117
  Overnight Chicken Casserole, 93
  Potato Salad, One-Gallon, 217
  Scrambled Egg Muffins, 35
  Sweet Potato Salad, 118
Eggnog, Safe Homemade, 194

**F**

Family picnics
  Banana Pepper Poppers, 200
  Chicken Meals, Campfire, 204
  Dustin's Skillet, 206
  Potato Sticks, Grilled or Baked, 205
  Shish Kabobs, Campfire, 203
  Supper on the Grill, 209
Family reunion meals
  Baked Beans, 212
  Chocolate Cake, 214
  Chocolate Chip Cookies, 213
  Potato Salad, One-Gallon, 217
  Scalloped Potatoes and Ham, 218
  Sweet Rolls, Mother's, 216
Filled Wiener Buns, 225
Finger Jigglers, 230
French Toast, Crunchy Crust, 36

Frostings and glazes
  Baked-On Frosting for Gingerbread Cookies, 149
  Caramel Cinnamon Roll Frosting, 56
  Cream Cheese Frosting, 156
  Filling for Whoopie Pies, 160
  for Frosted Banana Cake Bars, 133
  for Fruit Pizza, 174
  Glaze for Doughnuts, 44
  Icing for Pear Cake, 131
  Maple Sugar Frosting, 130
  Sauce for Caramel Dumplings, 46
Fruit
  Applesauce Cookies, 148
  Avocado Salsa, 186
  Banana Cake Bars, Frosted, 133
  Banana Cornbread Pancakes, 38
  Blueberry Cherry Supreme, 168
  Cherry Pie, 135
  Cobbler, Easy, 173
  Lemon Crisps, 154
  Lemon Pie, 136
  Oatmeal Pie, 139
  Peach Bread, 52
  Pear Cake, 131
  Pineapple Cookies, 155
  Pizza, 174
  Salad, Winter, 178
  Shish Kabobs, Campfire, 203
  Slush, 176
  Sour Cream Apple Pie, 142
  Strawberry Dip, 192
  Strawberry Pie Dessert, 180

## G

Garlic Bubble Loaf, 47
Garlic butter, 47
Garlic Dip, 187
Gelatin
  Finger Jigglers, 230
  Strawberry Pie Dessert, 180
Gingerbread Cookies, 149
Glaze. *See* Frostings and glazes
Goldenrod Eggs, 25
Goulash, Good, 87
Gravy
  Brown Butter Gravy, 109
  Hamburger Gravy, 113
Green Bean Casserole, 92
Ground beef
  Cabbage Rolls, 86
  Goulash, Good, 87
  Green Bean Casserole, 92
  Hamburger Gravy, 113
  Hamburger Soup, Hearty, 68
  Pizza Burgers, 75
  Spaghetti Casserole, Baked, 85
  Vegetable Soup, 69
  Zucchini Pizza Casserole, 100

## H

Ham
  Breakfast Brunch, 28
  Breakfast Casserole with White Sauce, 29
  Breakfast Omelet in a Skillet, 30
  Breakfast Omelet Roll, 32
  Cheesy Baked Eggs, 31
  Creamed Ham and Asparagus, 114
  Ham and Cabbage Soup, 66
  Ham and Cheese Sticky Buns, 76
  Scalloped Potatoes and Ham, 218
  Tortilla Roll-Ups, 231
Hamburger Gravy, 113
Hamburger Soup, Hearty, 68
Hot dogs, 225

## K

Kids, cooking with
  Cheesy Pretzels, 224
  Egg in the Nest, 226
  Filled Wiener Buns, 225
  Finger Jigglers, 230
  Pizza Bar Cookies, 229
  Tortilla Roll-Ups, 231

**L**

Lemon Crisps, 154
Lemon Pie, 136
Lettuce Salad, Layered, 117

**M**

Main dishes
  Barbecue Ribs, Baked, 82
  Cabbage Rolls, 86
  Chicken Casserole, Overnight, 93
  Chicken Hot Wings, 88
  Chicken Potpie, 91
  Goulash, Good, 87
  Green Bean Casserole, 92
  Pork 'n' Pepper Stir-Fry, 95
  Spaghetti Casserole, Baked, 85
  Sweet and Spicy Baked Chicken, 96
  Swiss Steak, 98
  Turkey Hash, 99
  Zucchini Pizza Casserole, 100
Maple Sugar Cake, 129
Maple Sugar Frosting, 130
Marinade, Meat, 191

Milk
  Bread Pie, Poor Man's, 143
  Cheese Soup, Mom's, 70
  Chicken Casserole, Overnight, 93
  Chocolate Pudding, 172
  Cream Puff Dessert, 171
  Eggnog, Safe Homemade, 194
  Hamburger Soup, Hearty, 68
  Peanut Butter Pudding, 177
  sauce for Goldenrod Eggs, 25
  Tomato Soup, 65
  Turkey Hash, 99
Molasses Cookies, Best, 150
Monkey Bread, 48
Muffins
  Morning Maple Muffins, 50
  Scrambled Egg Muffins, 35
Mushrooms. *See also* Cream of mushroom
    soup
  Dustin's Skillet, 206
  Shish Kabobs, Campfire, 203
  Supper on the Grill, 209
  Swiss Steak, 98
My Favorite Pizza Dough, 49

**N**

Nuts
  Applesauce Cookies, 148
  Cinnamon Pecan Coffee Cake,
    Overnight, 39
  Monkey Bread, 48
  Peanut Butter Pudding, 177
  Pecan Clusters, Toasted, 195
  Raggedy Top Bars, 162

**O**

Oatmeal Pie, 139
Omelets
  Breakfast Omelet in a Skillet, 30
  Breakfast Omelet Roll, 32
  Egg Omelet, 26
Onions
  Carrots and Onions, 112
  Dustin's Skillet, 206
  Shish Kabobs, Campfire, 203
  Supper on the Grill, 209
Overnight Cinnamon Pecan Coffee
  Cake, 39

**P**

Pancakes, Banana Cornbread, 38
Pasta dishes
  Chicken Casserole, Overnight, 93
  Coleslaw Pasta Salad, 122
  Goulash, Good, 87
  Green Bean Casserole, 92
  Spaghetti Casserole, Baked, 85
  Vegetable Soup, 69
Peach Bread, 52
Peanut Butter Pudding, 177
Pear Cake, 131
Peas
  Lettuce Salad, Layered, 117
Pecan Clusters, Toasted, 195

Peppers
  Avocado Salsa, 186
  Banana Pepper Poppers, 200
  Dustin's Skillet, 206
  Pork 'n' Pepper Stir-Fry, 95
  Salsa, Fresh, 188
  Shish Kabobs, Campfire, 203
  Supper on the Grill, 209
Pies, savory
  Chicken Potpie, 91
Pies, sweet
  Bread Pie, Poor Man's, 143
  Cherry, 135
  Lemon, 136
  Oatmeal, 139
  Pie Crust, 134
  Pumpkin, 140
  Sour Cream Apple, 142
  Strawberry Pie Dessert, 180
Pineapple
  Cookies, 155
  Shish Kabobs, Campfire, 203
Pizza, Fruit, 174
Pizza Bar Cookies, 229
Pizza Burgers, 75
Pizza Dough, My Favorite, 49
Poor Man's Bread Pie, 143
Pork
  Bacon and Egg Bake, 24
  Baked Beans, 212
  Barbecue Ribs, Baked, 82
  Breakfast Brunch, 28
  Breakfast Casserole with White Sauce, 29
  Breakfast Omelet in a Skillet, 30
  Breakfast Omelet Roll, 32
  Creamed Ham and Asparagus, 114
  Dustin's Skillet, 206
  Egg Omelet, 26
  Pizza Burgers, 75

Pork 'n' Pepper Stir-Fry, 95
Scalloped Potatoes and Ham, 218
Scrambled Egg Muffins, 35
Sloppy Joes, 74
Spaghetti Casserole, Baked, 85
Tortilla Roll-Ups, 231
Turkey Hash, 99
Zucchini Pizza Casserole, 100
Potatoes
  Autumn Vegetable Dish, 106
  Breakfast Casserole with White Sauce, 29
  Breakfast Omelet in a Skillet, 30
  Chicken Meals, Campfire, 204
  Potato Onion Cheese Soup, 73
  Potato Salad, One-Gallon, 217
  Potato Sticks, Grilled or Baked, 205

Ranch Potatoes, 116
Scalloped Potatoes and Ham, 218
Supper on the Grill, 209
Turkey Hash, 99
Potpie, Chicken, 91
Pudding
  Chocolate, 172
  Peanut Butter, 177
Pumpkin Brownies, 156
Pumpkin Cinnamon Rolls, 55
Pumpkin Pie, 140

**R**

Raggedy Top Bars, 162
Raisins
  Applesauce Cookies, 148
Ranch Potatoes, 116
Refrigerator Cookies, 157
Reunion meals
  Baked Beans, 212
  Chocolate Cake, 214
  Chocolate Chip Cookies, 213
  Potato Salad, One-Gallon, 217
  Scalloped Potatoes and Ham, 218
  Sweet Rolls, Mother's, 216
Rice
  Cabbage Rolls, 86
  Pork 'n' Pepper Stir-Fry, 95

**S**

Salads
  Coleslaw Pasta Salad, 122
  Fruit Salad, Winter, 178
  Lettuce Salad, Layered, 117
  Sweet Potato Salad, 118
  Zucchini Bean Salad, 121
Salsa
  Avocado, 186
  Fresh, 188
Sandwiches
  Filled Wiener Buns, 225
  Ham and Cheese Sticky Buns, 76
  Pizza Burgers, 75
  Sloppy Joes, 74
Sauces. *See* Dips and sauces
Sauerkraut
  Cabbage Rolls, 86
Scalloped Potatoes and Ham, 218
Scrambled Egg Muffins, 35
Shish Kabobs, Campfire, 203
Shrimp
  Dustin's Skillet, 206

Shish Kabobs, Campfire, 203
  Supper on the Grill, 209
Sloppy Joes, 74
Snowball Cookies, 158
Soups
  Bacon Bean, 64
  Cheese, Mom's, 70
  Ham and Cabbage, 66
  Hamburger, Hearty, 68
  Potato Onion Cheese, 73
  Tomato, 65
  Vegetable, 69
Sour Cream Apple Pie, 142
Spaghetti Casserole, Baked, 85
Squash
  Autumn Vegetable Dish, 106
  Pumpkin Brownies, 156
  Pumpkin Cinnamon Rolls, 55
  Pumpkin Pie, 140
  Zucchini Bean Salad, 121
  Zucchini Bread, 57
  Zucchini Pizza Casserole, 100
Stir-Fry, Pork 'n' Pepper, 95
Strawberry Dip, 192
Strawberry Pie Dessert, 180
Sugar Crumb Cake, 132
Supper on the Grill, 209
Sweet and Spicy Baked Chicken, 96
Sweet potatoes
  Autumn Vegetable Dish, 106
  Sweet Potato Salad, 118
Sweet Rolls, Mother's, 216
Swiss Steak, 98

**T**

Tomato dishes
　Avocado Salsa, 186
　Cabbage Rolls, 86
　Goulash, Good, 87
　Salsa, Fresh, 188
　Spaghetti Casserole, Baked, 85
　Tomato Soup, 65
　Vegetable Soup, 69
　Zucchini Pizza Casserole, 100
Tortilla Roll-Ups, 231
Turkey Hash, 99

**V**

Vegetable dishes. *See also specific vegetables*
　Autumn Vegetable Dish, 106
　Avocado Salsa, 186
　Bacon Fried Cabbage, 108
　Banana Pepper Poppers, 200
　Carrots and Onions, 112
　Coleslaw Pasta Salad, 122
　Creamed Ham and Asparagus, 114
　Lettuce Salad, Layered, 117
　Potato Onion Cheese Soup, 73
　Potato Salad, One-Gallon, 217
　Potato Sticks, Grilled or Baked, 205
　Ranch Potatoes, 116
　Salsa, Fresh, 188
　Sweet Potato Salad, 118
　Vegetable Bars, 110
　Vegetable Soup, 69
　Zucchini Bean Salad, 121
Venison
　Sloppy Joes, 74

**W**

White Bread, 58
Whoopie Pies, 161
Wiener Buns, Filled, 225
Winter Fruit Salad, 178

**Z**

Zucchini Bean Salad, 121
Zucchini Bread, 57
Zucchini Pizza Casserole, 100

## AUGUST 2000, ELIZABETH COBLENTZ

I miss my departed husband, Ben. He always put the hand-cranked juicer together and then turned it while I put in the jars to be processed. He also rinsed all the parts of the juicer at our water pump. He was helpful in so many ways. Ben put in hard-working days all the years of our marriage. He suffered a lot of asthma and hay fever during the summer, and often had pneumonia during the winter. Ben needed a lot of good care, and I was happy to give it to him. His parting is so hard, but God has a purpose for it all. He is the One who makes no mistakes.

*(Editor's note: Ben Coblentz passed away on May 14, 2000. More than seven hundred people attended his funeral.)*

## THE AUTHOR

Lovina Eicher is an Old Order Amish cook, mother, and author of *The Essential Amish Cookbook* and several other cookbooks. She writes the popular syndicated column Lovina's Amish Kitchen, which appears in thirty-six newspapers around the United States. Lovina and her husband, Joe, have eight children and five grandchildren. They live in rural Michigan.